END-TIME
TRUTHS
FOR END-TIME PEOPLE

END-TIME TRUTHS

TRUTHS

FOR END-TIME PEOPLE

THE TABERNACLE OF GOD'S GLORY AND THE
FESTIVALS OF JEHOVAH

CHARLES P. SCHMITT, D.MIN., D.D.

DESTINY IMAGE® PUBLISHERS, INC.
P.O. Box 310, Shippensburg, PA 17257-0310

"Speaking to the Purposes of God for This Generation and for the Generations to Come."

This book and all other Destiny Image, Revival Press, MercyPlace, Fresh Bread, Destiny Image Fiction, and Treasure House books are available at Christian bookstores and distributors worldwide.

For a U.S. bookstore nearest you, call **1-800-722-6774.**

For more information on foreign distributors, call **717-532-3040.**

Or reach us on the Internet: **www.destinyimage.com**

ISBN 10: 0-7684-3090-9

ISBN 13: 978-0-7684-3090-5

For Worldwide Distribution, Printed in the U.S.A.

1 2 3 4 5 6 7 8 9 10 11 / 13 12 11 10 09

ENDORSEMENTS

Jesus declared that the Scriptures of the Old Testament testify about Him. Philip asked the Ethiopian eunuch if he understood what he was reading, and the eunuch responded, "How could I, unless someone guides me?" It's amazing how much clearer the Scriptures are when someone like Dr. Charles Schmitt explains them to you. Recently, Pastor Charles spent three glorious days with our church "walking through the Bible," and the atmosphere was a revival! Pastor Charles is a pure teacher, and you will be captured by his insights into this wonderful message. As the Brits would say—this book is "brilliant!" Dr. Schmitt will guide you through the Tabernacle, and you will understand that it's all about Jesus!

—Joseph L. Garlington Sr.
Senior Pastor, Covenant Church of Pittsburgh
Presiding Bishop, Reconciliation Ministries International:
A Network of Churches and Ministries

I highly recommend Charles Schmitt's new book. This book is filled with revelation and end-time truths gleaned from the Tabernacle, the holy priesthood, and the festivals. Charles' new book is a joy to read as he leads us on a path that reveals the mysteries of Christ and His Church in the intricate designs of God's Golden House, the Tabernacle. The Festivals of Jehovah also come alive with revelation as the end-time work of our Lord Jesus is unveiled. Charles' book reveals how our Lord is preparing His people for His Return in a time of unparalleled outpouring and unprecedented ingathering in the earth! Expect to be both challenged and encouraged as you read each page of this amazing book.

—Larry Kreider
International Director
DOVE Christian Fellowship International

In this book, Charles captures the heart of God to redeem and live inside His people. He shares insights on the Tabernacle that have been birthed from a lifetime of faithful study and devotion to Him. Our willingness to house the presence of God will play a vital role in ushering in the return of Yeshua (Jesus).

—Asher Intrater
Director of Revive Israel Ministries, Jerusalem

I was very happy with this book. Charles Schmitt finds a wealth of spiritual meaning and rightly sees that the Church is like Israel by analogy, but does not replace the ethnic nation. Therefore the Tabernacle shows us much about the nature of the Church and spiritual life. It has high devotional quality as well.

—Daniel C. Juster
Director, Tikkun International

It is evident that the Holy Spirit used the pen of Charles Schmitt to reveal end-of-the-age mysteries. Charles' ability to put the magnifying glass on small details captured my attention through every chapter!

—John A. Kilpatrick
Brownsville Revival
Pastor, Church of His Presence, Daphne, Alabama

We live in an hour where God is preparing His people for the return of the King of kings, an hour of unparalleled outpouring and glorious harvest. We find shadows of these events reflected in the Tabernacle and the Festivals of Jehovah. I know few men who can share these exciting themes as well as Pastor Charles Schmitt. I commend this book as a valuable tool for understanding and guidance for His believing Church.

—Dr. Mahesh Chavda
Senior Pastor, All Nations Church

In this dynamic and insightful teaching, my friend Charles Schmitt offers seasoned insight and modern-day application for ancient Levitical worship. This book is for all those who desire to understand and enter into God's eternal patterns of worship!

—Robert Stearns
Executive Director
Eagles' Wings Ministries

TABLE OF CONTENTS

Opening Thoughts

THIS book is not intended to be an "easy read." Its contents cannot be lightly digested in one sitting. The details of the Tabernacle of God's Glory and the festivals of the Lord are divinely intricate beyond words! And so this book is written for the stouthearted who have a passion to uncover something more of "the depth of the riches of the wisdom and knowledge of God!" (Rom. 11:33). At times during the writing of this book I was so overwhelmed by God's Presence and by the illumination streaming from His Word that I could not put my pen down. I could only say with the psalmist, "My heart is stirred by a noble theme as I recite my verses for the king; my tongue is the pen of a skillful writer" (Ps. 45:1).

This book was written as part of the celebration of the 25th anniversary of Immanuel's Church, a very special expression of the Body of Christ in the Washington, D.C. area. These studies were actually first taught in Immanuel's School of Ministry before they were written down to become this book. The enthusiasm of my students along with the encouragements of my precious wife, Dotty, birthed the vision for this book.

I dedicate this book, which contains so much of the passion of my own heart, to my five grandchildren. As I wrote in the final words of Chapter 10: "The pursuit of the Presence of God [is] a generational legacy. I can only pray that my four grandsons, Chase Patrick and Kai Francis and Dylan Charles and Hunter Scott, and my lovely grand-daughter, Brooke Morgan, will also *walk habitually with God, 'ascending and descending'* in the Presence of God. That is the generational legacy I wish to leave behind!"

And so my grandchildren, I dedicate this book to *you*. Its message is my legacy to you. May you carry that message to your generation and to the generation that follows you, should Jesus tarry yet longer.

Finally, very sincere thanks to my faithful administrative assistant and secretary, Carol Wilkinson, who typed—and retyped and typed yet again—each page. And to Carol Griffith, who so faithfully proof-read each line—thank you! To Darlinda Sanders, my deep appreciation for your labor of love in creating the beautiful illustrations, and to Rosi and Wardell Parker and Herb Thomas for the artwork preparation. I am so grateful to you all. This is our joint labor of love for the Body of Christ!

Chapter 1

Two Golden Threads

THERE are two powerful themes that run as two golden threads throughout the whole of Holy Scripture; both themes have their beginnings in the Book of Genesis. The *messianic theme* of the Promised Redeemer begins in Genesis 3:15, at the very point of the fall of man, with a word given by God to satan: "…He [the Promised One] will crush your head, and you will strike His heel." This speaks of the mortal wound inflicted on the Promised One at His death, who by that very death would inflict a mortal wound on the serpent, satan, crushing his head, causing his undoing for all time and for all eternity!

This grand theme of the dying, triumphant Messiah runs throughout the whole of Holy Scripture, through hundreds of promises and pictures—in many types and many shadows—and by much prophetic pageantry, all pointing to One—our Lord Jesus Christ, "the Lamb of God, who takes away the sin of the world!" (John 1:29). The culmination of this glorious messianic theme is found in Revelation in the vision of "…a Lamb, looking as if it had been [freshly] slain, standing in the center of the throne…" (Rev. 5:6, lit.). The enthroned Lamb of God appears as Heaven's Darling, the center of all God's righteous rule, His bleeding wounds forever visible for the whole of creation to gaze upon in adoration and praise! Indeed, "Worthy is the Lamb, who was slain to receive [the] power and [the] wealth and [the] wisdom and

[the] strength and [the] honor and [the] glory and [the] praise!" (Rev. 5:12, lit.).

The second theme that runs as a golden thread so clearly throughout the whole of Holy Scripture is the theme of building *a house for our God to live in*. The quest to build a house for God started with that noble prophetic soul, Abraham. He was the first to rename the ancient city of Luz, Bethel, "the House of God." To the east of Bethel he pitched his tent and "…there he built an altar to the Lord and called on the name of the Lord" (Gen. 12:8). His vision was clearly to provide a house for God to dwell in, a place to meet with God.

This issue of a house for God to live in was not without its obvious problems. How *exactly* does one build a house for an omnipotent and infinite God who fills all of Heaven and all of earth? Solomon wrestled with this very issue: "Who is able to build a temple for Him, since the heavens, even the highest heavens, cannot contain Him?" (2 Chron. 2:6). And the Lord Himself enters into the discussion in Isaiah 66:1 when He declares, "…Heaven is My throne, and the earth is My footstool. *Where* is the house you will build for Me? *Where* will My resting place be?" And so the enigma exists—where can men house an infinite God? David seemed to find a plausible compromise. He had it in his heart "…to build a house…*for the footstool of our God…*" and so he "…made plans to build it" (1 Chron. 28:2). If it were impossible to house *all* of God, for the whole universe cannot contain Him, David would at least build a place to put God's *footstool:* a place where God could come and just kick off His shoes, so to speak, and put up His feet and be at home in the midst of His people.

I believe all of these word pictures present to us this second major theme of Holy Scripture. There is a passion within God's heart to dwell in the very midst of His people because He loves them and He has redeemed them! And there is a passion within God's people to have the near and abiding Presence of the God they have come to love and to adore!

If our Lord Jesus Christ is the first main theme of all Holy Scripture, then surely a house for our Lord Jesus Christ is its second main theme.

And these twin themes run as two golden threads throughout the length of God's Holy Word!

A HOUSE FOR GOD TO LIVE IN

Jacob's Stone

Jacob, the notorious grandson of Abraham, was the first builder to undertake providing a house for God. It would be a simple house made up of only one stone, and, of course, it would be built at Luz, the ancient city that his grandfather Abraham first prophetically renamed Bethel, the House of God.

As God revealed Himself to Jacob at Bethel, his response was: "How awesome is this place! This is none other than *the house of God..."* (Gen. 28:17). With that understanding:

> *Early the next morning Jacob took the stone he had placed under his head* [his pillow] *and set it up as a pillar and poured oil on top of it. He called that place Bethel* [the House of God], *though the city used to be called Luz* (Genesis 28:18-19).

This house was just a simple stone, but it was an *anointed* stone, and that was important, for the *anointing* would be the chief character-istic of God's house from this point forward. God's house would always be *an anointed house!*

Jacob declared, "This stone that I have set up as a pillar will be God's house, *and of all that You give me I will give You a tenth"* (Gen. 28:22). Hence, with God's house came immediate responsibility. Abraham, originator of the "House of God" concept, was the Bible's first tither (see Gen. 14:20). A revelation of God's house always results in the responsibility for the upkeep of that house! The poor and the needy would always need to be provided for in this house, since God is always inviting them as His guests. Also ministry to the Lord and to His people and to a lost world would arise from this house. Consequently, the tithe would make that all possible.

The Tabernacle of God's Glory

The next mention of a house for God was the Tabernacle of God's Glory, God's Mobile Home. In it He was to accompany Israel on their wilderness journey from Egypt to Canaan. "Have them make a sanctuary for Me, and *I will dwell among them*" (Exod. 25:8). Probably no house of God is as clearly detailed in all of its intricate design as *this* house. The Tabernacle was to be built according to the blueprint seen by Moses on the Mount. "Make this tabernacle and all its furnishings exactly like *the pattern I will show you*" (Exod. 25:9,40). "Set up the tabernacle according to *the plan shown you on the mountain*" (Exod. 26:30). Furthermore, Hebrews 8:5 tells us that the Tabernacle was *"a copy and shadow of what is in heaven."* The original Tabernacle is the *heavenly* reality, and comes to earth *from Heaven*.

God's heavenly original is our *Lord Jesus Himself.* John 1:14 provides us with this insight:

> *The Word became flesh and made His dwelling* [**tabernacled** (lit.)] *among us. We have seen His glory* [that same glory that would fill the Tabernacle and then later the Temple], *the glory of the One and Only, who came from the Father, full of grace and truth.*

In the Tabernacle of God's Glory we will, therefore, see amazing details about Jesus Himself and the intricate design of all He has come to accomplish for us. He, Himself, is the Dwelling Place of God, "For in *Christ* all the fullness of the Deity lives in bodily form" (Col. 2:9), "For God was pleased to have all His fullness *dwell in Him*" (Col. 1:19). Wonderful Lord Jesus!

But the Tabernacle of God is now more than the single Man, Jesus of Nazareth. Jesus of Nazareth has become the Head of *a Body*, "...the church, which is His body, the fullness of Him who fills everything in every way" (Eph. 1:22-23). So we now refer to Christ as the *"Corporate*

Christ," which is to say Jesus the Head, and the Church, His Body. The Church of our Lord Jesus Christ, His spotless Bride, is seen in Revelation 21:2 as "…coming down out of heaven from God, prepared as a bride beautifully dressed for her Husband." Thus the Church, the Bride of Christ, becomes "the Tabernacle of God," which is "…with men, and He will live with them" (Rev. 21:3). It is this corporate Christ—Jesus the Head and the Church, His Body—whom Moses saw in the blueprint on the holy mount. And Moses built the Tabernacle of God according to that plan, that pattern, that blueprint! In the Tabernacle we see the awesome mysteries of our Lord Jesus Christ and His Church!

The Tabernacle of David

The Tabernacle, or Tent, of David is referred to in Amos 9:11-12:

> *"In that day I will restore David's fallen tent. I will repair its broken places, restore its ruins, and build it as it used to be, so that they may possess the remnant of Edom and all the nations that bear My name," declares the Lord, who will do these things.*

God promised that He would restore and rebuild David's Tabernacle in the earth, using not only Israel but the Gentiles as building materials.

The apostle James understood Amos' words in exactly this way in Acts 15:13-19:

> *When they finished, James spoke up: "Brothers, listen to me. Simon has described to us how God at first showed His concern by taking from the Gentiles a people for Himself. The words of the prophets are in agreement with this, as it is written: 'After this I will return and rebuild David's fallen tent. Its ruins I will rebuild, and I will restore it, that the remnant of men may seek the Lord, and all the Gentiles who bear My name, says the Lord, who does these things' that have been known for ages."*

The Tabernacle of David, God's third house in Scripture, was not much more than a simple tent of worship that David provided to contain the Ark of God, a Holy of Holies to house the throne of His glorious Presence. There David, clothed in a linen ephod as a priest, worshiped and sacrificed "burnt offerings and peace offerings" to the Lord, and there David, in priestly fashion, "blessed the people in the name of the Lord" (1 Chron. 16:1-3). David had apparently begun to function in the Melchizedek priesthood, which came to him at the conquest of Melchizedek's ancient city, Salem, renamed *Jerusalem*. First Chronicles 11:4-5 states:

> *David and all the Israelites marched to Jerusalem (that is, Jebus). The Jebusites who lived there said to David, "You will not get in here." Nevertheless, David captured the fortress of Zion, the City of David.*

The Tabernacle of David is a study in holy, priestly, anointed simplicity—the adoration of a man deeply in love with His God! David speaks of the ecstasy of gazing "upon the beauty of the Lord" as he sought the Lord and as he inquired of Him in this rustic house of God—in "the shelter of His tabernacle" (Ps. 27:4-5).

The Temple of Jehovah

The elaborate plans for the glorious Temple of Jehovah, drawn from Moses' original blueprint, came from David himself. David also gathered the 3,750 tons of gold and the 37,500 tons of silver, plus all the other metals, wood, and stone for the Temple, valued today at over *$100 billion!*[1] According to First Chronicles 28:11-12:

> *David gave his son Solomon the plans for the portico of the temple, its buildings, its storerooms, its upper parts, its inner rooms and the place of atonement. He gave him the plans of all that the Spirit had put in his mind for the courts of the temple of the Lord and all the surrounding rooms, for the treasuries of the temple of God and for the treasuries for the dedicated things.*

David informed his son Solomon:

I have taken great pains to provide for the temple of the Lord a hundred thousand talents [3,750 tons] of gold, a million talents [37,500 tons] of silver, quantities of bronze and iron too great to be weighed, and wood and stone. And you may add to them (1 Chronicles 22:14).

Furthermore, David also helped assemble the 153,600 workmen who would labor seven years to complete the project in the early part of his son Solomon's reign (see 2 Chron. 2:1-2; 1 Kings 6:37-38). This was to be Jehovah's fourth house in Scripture—and it was a magnificent house filled with the Glory of God!

The Restoration Temple of Zerubbabel

The Book of Second Chronicles, however, closes on a very painful note. Because of the sin and the waywardness of God's people, God allowed Solomon's magnificent Temple to be destroyed some 400 years after it was built. The armies of Nebuchadnezzar, emperor of Babylon, tore it to the ground and burned it with fire.

The Lord, the God of their fathers, sent word to them through His messengers again and again, because He had pity on His people and on His dwelling place. But they mocked God's messengers, despised His words and scoffed at His prophets until the wrath of the Lord was aroused against His people and there was no remedy. He brought up against them the king of the Babylonians, who killed their young men with the sword in the sanctuary, and spared neither young man nor young woman, old man or aged. God handed all of them over to Nebuchadnezzar...They set fire to God's temple and broke down the wall of Jerusalem; they burned all the palaces and destroyed everything of value there (2 Chronicles 36:15-17;19).

But the restoration of a house for God, the fifth such dwelling for God in Holy Scripture, dominates the scene in the very next book, the Book of Ezra. Cyrus, the king of Persia, had decreed:

> Anyone of His people among you—may his God be with him, and let him go up to Jerusalem in Judah and build the temple of the Lord, the God of Israel, the God who is in Jerusalem (Ezra 1:3).

Under the prophetic encouragement of the prophets Haggai and Zechariah, a restoration temple was completed by Zerubbabel, the appointed Jewish governor, and Joshua (Jeshua) the High Priest.

> Now Haggai the prophet and Zechariah the prophet, a descendant of Iddo, prophesied to the Jews in Judah and Jerusalem in the name of the God of Israel, who was over them. Then Zerubbabel son of Shealtiel and Jeshua son of Jozadak set to work to rebuild the house of God in Jerusalem. And the prophets of God were with them, helping them (Ezra 5:1-2).

Because of the opposition, it took all of 20 years to complete.[2] The whole restoration scenario found in Ezra, Nehemiah, Haggai, and Zechariah becomes for us today a picture of our Lord's present passion to recover His people from their spiritual Babylonian captivity and to restore His Church as His house, the dwelling place of His Presence in the earth!

Nonetheless, one solemn fact stands out in the restoration Temple of Zerubbabel—no glory fell as it did on the Tabernacle of God and on Solomon's magnificent Temple. Actually, there was no Ark of the Covenant in the Holy of Holies! Some scholars believe that the Ark was last in the hands of Jeremiah the prophet and was hidden by him as stated in the apocryphal writing Second Maccabees 2:4-8; it has not been found to this day. Without the Ark, there could be no glory, for the glory cloud was to rest between the glorious cherubim. However, the following amazing prophecy from the Lord was given through Haggai the prophet:

*"I will shake all nations, and the desired of all nations **will come, and I will fill this house with glory,**" says the Lord Almighty.... "The glory of this present house will be greater than the glory of the former house," says the Lord Almighty. "And in this place I will grant peace," declares the Lord Almighty* (Haggai 2:7,9).

That great prophecy would find its fulfillment in the person of our Lord Jesus Christ Himself.

Our Lord Jesus Christ

The ultimate dwelling place of God—the Man, Christ Jesus—is the fulfillment of all that prefigured Him, and in Him, the Man of Peace, Haggai's prophecy was literally fulfilled. All scholars agree that the Temple in which Jesus walked and worshiped and taught was Zerubbabel's original Temple, though expanded and embellished by Herod the Great. Into that Temple came the One who is the Desired of all nations, the One in whom *all* the fullness of God's glory dwelt, and from whom, on that greater temple site, would be poured out a manifestation of the Shekinah Glory of God on the Day of Pentecost that would literally shake all nations to their foundations! Haggai's prophecy was clearly fulfilled in the Person of our Lord Jesus, though the final installment of Haggai's profound prophecy will *yet* come to pass in these last days through Christ Jesus our Lord, according to Hebrews 12:26-29:

At that time His voice shook the earth, but now He has promised, "Once more I will shake not only the earth but also the heavens." The words "once more" indicate the removing of what can be shaken—that is, created things—so that what cannot be shaken may remain. Therefore, since we are receiving a kingdom that cannot be shaken, let us be thankful, and so worship God acceptably with reverence and awe, for our "God is a consuming fire."

The Body of Christ

Paul makes a most unusual statement in First Corinthians 12:12-13:

> The body is a unit, though it is made up of many parts; and though all its parts are many, they form one body. **So it is with Christ.** For we were all baptized by one Spirit into one body—whether Jews or Greeks, slave or free—and we were all given the one Spirit to drink.

Here Paul refers to the Church as *"the Christ"* in his statement: "So it is with *the Christ*" (lit.). Clearly, Jesus is the Head and His Church is His Body, and this union—the Head and the Body—is God's *corporate Christ*, God's many-membered Man. Paul likewise makes it very plain that the Church, the corporate Christ, is the dwelling place of our God:

> Built on the foundation of the apostles and prophets, with Christ Jesus Himself as the chief cornerstone. In Him the whole building is joined together and rises to become **a holy temple in the Lord.** And in Him you too are being built together to become **a dwelling in which God lives by His Spirit** (Ephesians 2:20-22).

The Church collectively is God's Temple, but so also is the Church in all of its individual parts. In First Corinthians 6:19, Paul stresses this point by asking the individual believer, "Do you not know that your body is a temple of the Holy Spirit, who is in you, whom you have received from God? You are not your own." And in First Corinthians 3:16, Paul asks believers collectively: "Don't you know that you yourselves are God's temple and that God's Spirit lives in you?"

The Holy City, the New Jerusalem

The culmination of all that God has been after through the millennia of biblical history, with all its types and shadows, is simply this—a triumphant people, headed up by Christ, and joined as one to Christ, as totally as a man is joined to his wife—a people impregnated and "...filled to the measure of all the fullness of God" (Eph. 3:19). And this is the vision that John sees in Revelation 21. Here the bride, the wife of the Lamb is seen as "the tabernacle of God..." (Rev. 21:3 NKJV). Here the Lord God Almighty and the Lamb are the temple of God (see Rev. 21:22).

The corporate Christ, consisting of Jesus the Head and the Church His Body, is the ultimate house for God to live in. All the types and shadows of the past are fulfilled in the glorified Jesus and His glorified Church! All that Jacob's stone and the Tabernacle of Moses and the Tent of David and the magnificent Temple of Solomon and the restoration Temple of Zerubbabel spoke about are fulfilled in the Christ. Our Lord Jesus and His Body are the Tabernacle of God, the Temple of the living God, filled with God's awesome Presence! And so it shall be, with all His enemies beneath His feet, that our God shall eternally reign as supreme, for "When He has done this [subjected all His enemies], then the Son Himself will be made subject to Him who put everything under Him, *so that God may be all in all*" (1 Cor. 15:28).

The exciting days in which we live are witnessing a passion within the hearts of many of God's people for a restoration of God's house in all the earth. These are days of divine recovery as God is moving everywhere by His Spirit! Because of the unusual Pentecostal century that we have just concluded, the Kingdom of God has exploded in the earth, making the Christian faith of 2 billion followers of Jesus the strongest faith in all the world, nearly twice the size of the next largest religion, Islam, with its over 1.2 billion people.[3]

These unusual outpourings of the Holy Spirit all across the face of the earth from the 20th century are now spilling over into the next century, bringing with them a passion for the restoration of the Church. And God is indeed giving Jesus the power to raise up His Body in a most wonderful way in these last days—all in preparation for Jesus' awesome return. The restoration of the Presence of God, the restoration of worship and adoration, the restoration of apostolic witness, the restoration of the gifts and ministries of the Holy Spirit, the restoration of signs and wonders, the restoration of divine order, the restoration of Israel to the Body of Christ—all are parts of God's restoration of His house!

In the recovery of Israel alone, as God pours out His Spirit on the remnant of His ancient people, "all Israel will be saved!" (Rom. 11:26; see Zech. 13:8-9 as to how this will come about). Peter had prophesied that God would continue to send "times of refreshing...from the Lord" (Acts 3:19) upon His people for the express purpose:

> *That He may* [then] *send the Christ, who has been appointed for you—even Jesus* [who] *must remain in heaven until the time comes for God* **to restore everything,** *as He promised long ago through His holy prophets* (Acts 3:20-21).

We can believe that these times are those of recovery and restoration of all that has been lost, which will then trigger the return of our Lord.

James had prophetically spoken of the last days, the days of "the Lord's coming," as days in which the heavenly Husbandman "waits for the land to yield its valuable crop and how patient He is for the autumn [early] and spring [latter] rains" to fall from heaven making that grand harvest possible (James 5:7). Peter, in quoting Joel, had prophetically declared:

> *In the last days, God says, I will pour out My Spirit on all people. Your sons and daughters will prophesy, your young men will see visions, your old men will dream dreams...I will show wonders in the heaven above and signs on the earth below...before the coming of the great and glorious day of the Lord. And **everyone** who calls on the name of the Lord will be saved* (Acts 2:17;19-21).

The last days, accompanied by tremendous outpourings of the Holy Spirit, with gifts and manifestations, signs and wonders, are destined to see the greatest harvest of souls ever! In Greek, Acts 2:21 literally reads: "It will be *everyone*, whoever calls on the name of the Lord, who will be saved." John, in Revelation 7:9, saw the vastness of that end-time harvest. Along with the sealed of Israel (see Rev. 7:4) he saw "a great multitude *that no one could count,* from every nation, tribe, people and language...." Referring to the harvest, Peter in his second letter comments on the reason for Jesus' delay. In actuality, His tarrying is only a few days on God's calendar, though several thousands of years on ours. Peter assures us that it is only because of the Lord's "not wanting *anyone* to perish, but *everyone* to come to repentance." And in the midst of this prophetic challenge to us, Peter pointedly admonishes us: "What kind of people ought you to be? You ought to live holy and godly lives *as you look forward to the day of God and speed its coming...*"! (2 Pet. 3:8-9;11-12).

In this awesome restoration, we are all invited to play a part. It is within our hand, by our obedience, and by our consecration, to hurry, to hasten, to speed, to accelerate the coming of our Lord Jesus Christ. In these last days by God's grace, *we will rise up* in the strength of our Lord Jesus Christ to do exactly that!

Prayer of Consecration

Father, I offer myself "a living sacrifice" on Your holy altar of consecration. Take my life, in the Name of our Lord Jesus Christ, and use it to speed along the coming of the day of God. Amen!

Endnote

1. The NIV footnote to First Chronicles 22:14 states that 100,000 talents of gold is "about 37,500 tons" (or 120 million ounces). At nearly $1,000 an ounce, the gold alone would be worth over *$120 billion* in today's values.

2. Work on the Temple began in 538 B.C. and was completed in 516 B.C., according to the NIV Study Bible notes on page 674 and 678.

3. The updated *Operation World* puts the total number of
    Christians at 1.97 billion, and the number of those adhering to
    Islam at 1.28 billion in 2004 (p. 2).

Chapter 2

THE TABERNACLE—
THE MEETING PLACE

THE expression, "the Tent of Meeting," which describes the Tabernacle, appears 144 times in Holy Scripture. The intent of God in the Tabernacle is clear—God desires to *meet with His people!* "I will *meet* with you...," the Lord eagerly tells Moses in Exodus 25:22. The original tent, which was erected before the Tabernacle was formally built, was itself called *the tent of meeting.* "...Anyone inquiring of the Lord would go to *the tent of meeting...* [There] the Lord would speak

artwork by Pat Marvenko Smith©2000—for artprints go to www.revelationillustrated.com

to Moses face to face, as a man speaks with his friend..." and there young Joshua, Moses' successor, would linger in the abiding Presence of Jehovah (Exod. 33:7,11). This was to become the main purpose for the Tabernacle of God's glory—the Meeting Place!

The next several chapters of this study are devoted to the intricate detail of the Tabernacle, this most wonderful meeting place of God, a place where God dwelt and a place where He met with His people. The Tabernacle's symbols are important to us because the details of the Tabernacle are carried forward and amplified in the houses that would follow: the Tent of David, Solomon's Temple, and Zerubbabel's restoration Temple. The one salient feature of Jacob's stone, which preceded the Tabernacle built by Moses, will also be carried forward and magnified in the Tabernacle. The Tabernacle would be *an anointed house*, as would be all of the dwellings that followed. On this backdrop then, let us now examine the outer courts of the Tabernacle.

THE OUTER COURTS OF THE TABERNACLE

—"SUCH A GREAT SALVATION" (Hebrews 2:3)

Psalm 84 is a passionate psalm that celebrates the dwelling place of God and the beauty of the courts of the Lord, the outer courts in particular.

> *How lovely is **Your dwelling place**, O Lord Almighty! My soul yearns, even faints, for **the courts of the Lord...a place near Your altar,** O Lord Almighty, my King and my God. Blessed are those who dwell in **Your house**; they are ever praising You. Selah...Better is one day in **Your courts** than a thousand elsewhere; I would rather be a doorkeeper in **the house of my God** than dwell in the tents of the wicked (Psalm 84:1-4;10).*

As we examine the outer courts of the Tabernacle, may our hearts be as deeply stirred as the psalmist's, for here we see clear and vivid pictures of what Hebrews 2:3 calls "such a great salvation!"

THE OUTER COURTS—A PLACE OF RESTRICTION

Exodus 27:9-19 describes the restricting, even forbidding, outer courts of the Tabernacle. The "courtyard," as it is called, was 150 feet long by 75 feet wide, half the size of a modern day football field. The perimeters of this courtyard on the north, south, east, and west were defined by 450 feet of "curtains of finely twisted linen" (27:9) that stood 7½ feet high, hung with silver hooks on 60 posts capped with silver and stabilized in 60 bronze bases all the way around the 450 feet of the courtyard.

Several things stand out concerning this courtyard. First of all, we notice these 450 feet of curtains made of dazzling white, finely twisted linen, measuring 7½ feet high and forming the basic footprint of the holy courtyard. "Fine linen, bright and clean" is a picture in Holy Scripture of the awesome righteousness a righteous God *requires* of His people. In Revelation 19:8 and 14, God *gives*, as a gift of His grace, "fine linen, bright and clean" to His Church, their only acceptable wedding garments. These 450 feet of linen curtains in the courtyard speak to us of God's holy standard of righteousness for His people. These curtains were 7½ feet high—too high to allow anyone to enter by climbing over and too high for anyone even to *see* over! In all their dazzling white brilliance the curtains actually *prevented* people's entrance. The bronze bases, likewise, forbid people from crawling under the curtains to gain entrance. Burnished bronze is a symbol in Scripture of the righteous judgments of God against sin (see Rev. 1:15; 14:19-20; 19:15). There were fully 2½ tons of brass used in the construction of the Tabernacle (see Exod. 38:29-31), most of it found in these bronze bases in the courtyard.

Silver is the metal of redemption, the coin of ransom. According to Exodus 30:11-16:

> *Then the Lord said to Moses, "When you take a census of the Israelites to count them, each one must pay the Lord a ransom for his life at the time he is counted. Then no plague will come on them when you number them [as happened*

in Second Samuel 24]...*those twenty years old or more are to give an offering to the Lord. The rich are not to give more than a half shekel and the poor are not to give less when you make the offering to the Lord to atone for your lives. Receive the atonement money from the Israelites and use it for the service of the Tent of Meeting. It will be a memorial for the Israelites before the Lord, making atonement for your lives.*"

And Exodus 38:25-28 tells us that about 3¾ tons of this silver were used in the construction of the Tabernacle, about 45 pounds just for the silver hooks, caps, and bands on the 60 posts on which the curtains hung. The restricting high curtains and the forbidding bronze bases that supported the posts carried with them the promise—the promise of redemption, of ransom, as clearly seen in the silver hooks and caps and bands on these posts.

Curtains so high that one cannot enter or even see over remind us of God's sober indictment against all humanity—"For all have sinned and *fall short* of the glory of God" (Rom. 3:23). In that verdict we are confronted with the truth that "no one can *enter* the kingdom of God," nor can even *"see* the kingdom of God unless he is *born again"* (John 3:3,5). The courtyard declares loudly and clearly, "You must be born again" (John 3:7)! That brings us to our next insight of the outer courts.

THE OUTER COURTS—A PLACE OF INVITATION

On the east side facing the sunrise, the Lord provided an entrance, an abundant entrance, all of 30 feet wide, embroidered with "blue, purple and scarlet yarn and finely twisted linen," hung on four posts resting in four bronze bases (see Exod. 27:13,16). This wide entrance, or gate, is a picture of our sufficient Lord Jesus Christ who declared: "*I am* the way and the truth and the life. No one comes to the Father except *through Me*" (John 14:6). "*I am* the gate; whoever enters *through Me* will be saved..." (John 10:9). And everyone who attempts to climb in by some other way will be found to be "a thief and a robber" (John 10:1).

The colors in this wide 30-foot embroidered gate are not difficult to understand. They all speak of the character of Jesus, as strands of blue, purple, and scarlet yarn were woven into the 30-foot finely twisted linen curtain. The color blue, extracted from blue shellfish from the Red Sea, speaks of the *heavenly* character of our Lord Jesus. This is the theme of John's Gospel. The royal color purple, extracted from the purple snail, *murex*, speaks of His *kingly* character, the theme of Matthew's Gospel. The color scarlet, extracted from crushing the worm *coccus ilicis*, speaks of Jesus' lowly, sacrificial character. He is the "*worm...* scorned by men and despised by the people" (Ps. 22:6), "*crushed* for our iniquities" (Isa. 53:5), which is the theme of Mark's Gospel. At this juncture, it is important to remember that the redemption cord that the spies gave to Rahab the harlot was a cord of "*scarlet*," the same Hebrew word used here (see Josh. 2:18). Rahab was to hang this "scarlet cord" from her window, as her personal "Passover" celebration, for the Lord promised her, in effect, "when I see the blood, I will pass over you" (Exod. 12:13). Finally, the white linen speaks of Jesus' righteous and spotless character, the theme of Luke's Gospel. Indeed, in all of His aspects, "He is altogether lovely," "outstanding among ten thousand" (Song of Sol. 5:16,10). And He Himself is our sufficient point of entrance into the Kingdom of God!

This embroidered curtain was held high on four posts, set in four bases of bronze—a symbol of the four Gospels declaring to the four corners of the world, "from east to west the sacred and imperishable message of eternal salvation" (words taken from an ancient conclusion to the Gospel of Mark).

The message of the wide multicolored gate is plain and it is simple— "Come to Me, all you who are weary and burdened, and *I* will give you rest!" (Matt. 11:28). Lord Jesus, I come!

The Outer Courts—A Place of Redemption

Other world religions begin their journey toward God by washings. I have watched Hindus washing themselves before they enter their temples of worship. I have watched Muslims washing themselves before they enter their mosques. The Tabernacle, likewise, has a place for washing, but *it does not come first*. Unlike other world religions, our very first experience as we seek to enter God's Presence to worship is to experience *the blood atonement!*

Just inside the vast gate of entrance stands the bronze altar of burnt offering. According to Exodus 27:1-8, the bronze altar was made of acacia wood overlaid with bronze. Acacia wood, a durable species of mimosa, is a symbol of Jesus' humanity. This wood was overlaid with bronze, a symbol of God's righteous judgment against sin—hammered upon the humanity of our Lord Jesus Christ as He, "the root out of dry ground" took up our infirmities and carried our sorrows, "pierced for our transgressions...crushed for our iniquities..." (Isa. 53:2,4-5).

The bronze altar stood 4½ feet high and was 7½ feet long and 7½ feet wide. This altar was in essence a hollow box (see Exod. 27:8), believed to be elevated on a low mound of earth to allow for an updraft as the wood was burned inside at the base of the altar. Also, "a grating...a bronze network" was placed inside "halfway up the altar," (Exod. 27:4-5) and on this grating was placed the atoning sacrifices.

Because of the updraft, the hottest point of the consuming fire was at that grating "halfway up the altar." As a person looked at the altar, they would not be able to see that hottest point of the consuming fire for it was hidden inside halfway up the altar. God, looking down upon the altar from above, however, would see that point, but not man. This is a foreshadowing of the significance of the earth being shrouded in darkness from the sixth hour until the ninth hour (see Luke 23:44-45), concealing from men the deepest agonies of the Son of Man as He was made an atonement for our sin on the cross. *This was seen only by His Father looking down from above!*

The bronze altar was called the altar of "Continuous Burnt Offering." The Lord commanded:

> *Every morning the priest is to add firewood and arrange the burnt offering on the fire and burn the fat of the fellowship offerings on it. **The fire must be kept burning on the altar continuously; it must not go out** (Leviticus 6:12-13).*

Each morning and each evening, according to Exodus 29:38-39, a spotless lamb was offered on the altar, a symbol of Jesus, "the Lamb of God, who takes away the sin of the world" (John 1:29). Because of the atonement, and *only* because of the atonement, men and women could then meet with God!

> *…This burnt offering is to be made regularly* [continually] *at the entrance to the Tent of Meeting before the Lord. **There** I will **meet you and speak** to you…and the place will be **consecrated by My glory** (Exodus 29:42-43).*

According to Leviticus 1:4, the format for the burnt offering was clear: "He is to lay his hand on the head of the burnt offering, and it will be *accepted on his behalf* to make atonement for him." This animal was to die as an acceptable offering in place of the offender. In the case of the "goat of removal" on the Day of Atonement the ritual came into even sharper focus:

> *He is to lay both hands on the head of the live goat and confess over it all the wickedness and rebellion of the Israelites—all*

*their sins—**and put them on the goat's head...*** (Leviticus 16:21).

These sacrificial animals were *substitutes,* symbolically carrying the sins of the offender upon themselves. How clearly this speaks to us of the substitutionary death of our Lord Jesus Christ: "He Himself bore our sins in His body on the tree, so that we might die to sins and live for righteousness; by His wounds you have been healed" (1 Pet. 2:24). "God made Him who had no sin to be sin for us, so that in Him we might become the righteousness of God" (2 Cor. 5:21). At the four corners of the altar of bronze were also four "horns" of bronze. Psalm 118:27 (NKJV) sheds light on their function: "...Bind the sacrifice with cords to the horns of the altar," a symbol of the utter and irretractable sacrifice of our Lord Jesus on the cross!

Finally, the Lord commanded, "Make *poles* of acacia wood for the altar and overlay them with bronze. The poles are to be inserted into the rings so they will be on two sides of the altar when it is carried" (Exod. 27:6-7). The bronze altar was to be *mobile;* it was to be carried by the priests on their journey, a picture of the great commission—*"Go into all the world* and preach the good news *to all creation"* (Mark 16:15). And the "good news" is this:

> *When Christ came as high priest...He did not enter by means of the blood of goats and calves; but He entered the Most Holy Place **once for all by His own blood,** having obtained eternal redemption...He has appeared **once for all** at the end of the ages to do away with sin by the sacrifice of Himself* (Hebrews 9:11-12;26).

Praise God!

Our own personal response to such amazing love, that which would cause our Lord Jesus to die for us, is expressed in Romans 12:1, a further reference to the altar of burnt offering: "I urge you...in view of God's mercy, to *offer your bodies as living sacrifices,* holy and pleasing to God—this is your spiritual act of worship." What else could we ever do in the face of such amazing love?

THE OUTER COURTS—A PLACE OF CLEANSING

The following describes the final article in the outer courtyard—the bronze basin, or laver:

> *Then the Lord said to Moses, "Make a bronze basin, with its bronze stand, for washing. Place it between the Tent of Meeting and the altar, and put water in it. Aaron and his sons are to wash their hands and feet with water from it. Whenever they enter the Tent of Meeting, they shall wash with water so that they will not die. Also, when they approach the altar to minister by presenting an offering made to the Lord by fire, they shall wash their hands and feet so that they will not die. This is to be a lasting ordinance for Aaron and his descendants for the generations to come."* (Exodus 30:17-21)

Furthermore, "they made the bronze basin and its bronze stand from *the mirrors of the women* who served at the entrance to the Tent of Meeting" (Exod. 38:8). These women traded their human beauty for the divine beauty that comes from gazing intently into the mirrored waters of the bronze laver, perhaps alluded to in James 1:23-25:

> *Anyone who listens to the word but does not do what it says is like a man who looks at his face in a mirror and, after looking at himself, goes away and immediately forgets what he looks like. But the man who looks intently into the perfect law that gives freedom, and continues to do this, not forgetting what he has heard, but doing it—he will be blessed in what he does.*

The initial use of this bronze basin is stated in Exodus 29:4-5: "Bring Aaron and his sons to the entrance to the Tent of Meeting and *wash them* with water. [Then] take the garments and dress Aaron...." If words mean anything, we can believe that Aaron and his sons, standing unclothed in the Presence of the Lord, were washed with pure water before they were clothed in their priestly robes. Hebrews 10:22 sheds light for us on this symbolic act in these words:

Let us draw near to God with a sincere heart in full assurance of faith, having our hearts sprinkled to cleanse us from a guilty conscience and having our bodies washed with pure water.

The reference is clearly to the repentant believer being "buried with [Christ] in baptism and raised with Him through…faith in the power of God, who raised Him from the dead" (Col. 2:12). As an interesting side note, the basin or laver in Solomon's Temple was called "The Sea" and held all of 17,500 gallons of water (see 2 Chron. 4:4-5); it was the size of a modern day swimming pool, or a large baptismal!

The ongoing use of the bronze basin was for *daily* cleansing, for continued "…washing with water through the word" (Eph. 5:26). "Aaron and his sons are to *wash their hands and feet* with water…Whenever they enter the Tent of Meeting, they shall wash with water so that they will not die…" (Exod. 30:19-20). Indeed, "…Who may stand in His holy place? He who has *clean hands* and a pure heart…He will receive blessing from the Lord…" (Ps. 24:3-5). Lord, may this be true of *me!*

CONCLUSION

The outer courts of the Tabernacle unfold for us "such a great salvation," and, in the process, raise important questions before our eyes. Have I been born again that I might both see and enter the Kingdom of God? Have I entered God's Kingdom through Christ, the wide Gate? Have I trusted the power of Christ's sufficient atoning blood for my cleansing, for the forgiveness of sins? Have I gone down in the "Sea" of God's forgetfulness, having my body washed with pure water? Do I daily wash my soiled hands and feet, looking into the mirrored reflection of God's Holy Word, coming away changed?

As we stand amazed in the outer courts, we rejoice with David:

Blessed are those You choose and bring near to live in Your courts! We are filled with the good things of Your house… (Psalm 65:4).

Amen!

PRAYER OF CONSECRATION

Lord Jesus Christ, I thank You for "such a great salvation" that You have so graciously provided *for me* in Your death and burial and resurrection! And I affirm, by faith in You, that I *do* receive with joy, Your saving grace into my life! I *do* receive Your gracious forgiveness! I *do* receive the gift of God, eternal life, from Your hand! Thank You for saving me, and thank You for keeping me! In Your precious Name. Amen.

Chapter 3

THE TABERNACLE—FITLY FRAMED AND KNIT TOGETHER

SPEAKING of the Church, Paul writes:

> *In* [Jesus] *the whole building is joined together* ["fitly framed together," KJV]...*and in Him you too are being built together to become a dwelling in which God lives by His Spirit* (Ephesians 2:21-22).

> *United in love* ["knit together in love," KJV]...*the whole body...held together* ["knit together," KJV]...*grows as God causes it to grow* (Colossians 2:2,19).

The construction of the Tabernacle so beautifully typified these truths as Moses outlined the God-given pattern for the ten *curtains,* the *coverings,* the *boards,* the *veil,* and the *entrance* to the Tent of Meeting. In these construction materials and how they were joined together, we see the Church "fitly framed together" and "knit together" in Christ and in His amazing love!

The Ten Curtains of Fine Linen (Exodus 26:1-6)

The Tent of Meeting itself was made of "ten curtains of finely twisted linen and blue, purple and scarlet yarn, with cherubim worked into them by a skilled craftsman" (Exod. 26:1). These ten curtains were the inmost covering of the house of gold draped over the walls of the Holy Sanctuary, the gold covered boards (which we will shortly consider).

The white linen of the ten curtains speaks to us of Jesus' spotless *righteousness,* which has now become ours by His grace:

> It is because of Him that you are in Christ Jesus, who has **become for us** wisdom from God—that is, **our righteousness,** holiness and redemption (1 Corinthians 1:30).

> God made Him who had no sin to be sin for us, so that in Him we might become **the righteousness of God** (2 Corinthians 5:21).

> Fine linen, bright and clean, was given her to wear (Revelation 19:8) (*Fine linen* stands for the righteous acts ["**the righteousness,**" KJV] of the saints.)

The blue strands of yarn speak of Jesus' *heavenly* life, which we now also share by His grace, as we are "seated...with Him in the *heavenly realms* in Christ Jesus" (Eph. 2:6).

The purple strands speak to us of Jesus' royal kingship and of us who have been made by Him "*a kingdom* and priests to serve His God and Father..." (Rev. 1:6).

The scarlet strands of yarn tell us of His *redemption,* which also has now been given to us by His grace. He "has *become for us...redemption*" (1 Cor. 1:30).

The new addition to these linen curtains (beyond the curtains of the outer court) are the "*cherubim* worked into them by a skilled craftsman" (Exod. 26:1), which speaks to us of the ongoing ministry of angels in the Church: "Are not all angels *ministering* spirits sent to *serve* those who will inherit salvation?" (Heb. 1:14).

One of the Colossian Gnostic errors was "the *worship* of angels" (Col. 2:18); but one of our modern day errors is *overlooking* these same angels. We need a fresh consciousness of angels and their ministry to us, without an unhealthy fixation on them. We need a fresh revelation of angelic interventions in our lives. We need a fresh expectancy of their ministry on our behalf. Our Lord Jesus has a personal angel (see Rev. 1:1). Little children have protecting angels (see Matt. 18:10). Saints have attending angels (see Acts 12:15; Heb. 1:14). Churches have angels (see Rev. 2:1,8,12,18; 3:1,7,14). And the end-time Israel of God has a strong protecting angel, Michael (see Dan. 12:1). How wonderful is the ministry of angels to the people of God!

Each of the ten curtains was to be 42 feet long and 6 feet wide (see Exod. 26:2), and these huge ten curtains were to be fastened together by 50 gold clasps "so that the tabernacle is *a unit* ['it shall be *one* tabernacle']" (Exod. 26:6 KJV). Gold is the metal that speaks of the nature of God Himself, and "50" is the number of Pentecost (the *fiftieth* day after Passover). Scripture describes the Pentecostal blessing in these words: "For we were *all baptized by one Spirit* into one body..." (1 Cor. 12:13). By means of the work of the Spirit of God, we, the Church, have been clasped together as one body, "...*built together* to become a dwelling in which God lives by His Spirit" (Eph. 2:22)! In view of all that God has done in joining us together, we must indeed "make every effort to *keep the unity of the Spirit* through the bond of peace." And to that end we are to "be completely humble and gentle...patient, bearing with one another in love" (Eph. 4:2-3).

Unfortunately, today there are many professing Christians who are in fellowship with no one. They are not "knit together" with anyone. Some "worship God on the golf course," which we should do; we should worship Him at all times and in every place! Others attend "Cyber Church," which is a good supplement but a poor substitute for gathering together. We need the anointed experience of "church" as well. Consistent gathering together in the Name of Jesus with other believers is *essential* to the health of our souls!

In Hebrews, a book that speaks so much on Tabernacle themes, we are admonished: "Let us not give up meeting together, as some are in the habit of doing, but let us encourage one another—and all the more as you see the Day approaching" (Heb. 10:25). It is easy to develop a *habit* of not gathering together. The pressures of life, the call of material things, our own laziness, all contribute to developing this hurtful habit. Sometimes bad experiences in church can contribute to our delinquency, but we need to learn to forgive.

Others neglect gathering together because it is lifeless and irrelevant to them, but we need to seek out a living, relevant expression of Christ's Body! "And all the more as you see the Day approaching" (Heb. 10:25)! The end-times bring with them pressure and peril—"Be careful, or your hearts will be weighed down...and that day will close on you unexpectedly like a trap" (Luke 21:34). We need the encouragement of the Body of Christ: "Encourage one another daily, as long as it is called Today, so that none of you may be hardened by sin's deceitfulness" (Heb. 3:13). This is the lesson we see in these Tabernacle curtains all being held together by the 50 clasps of gold. This is the Church "joined together...to become a dwelling in which God lives by His Spirit" (Eph. 2:21-22). This is the Body of Christ "held together" and growing as God causes it to grow (see Col. 2:19). God is requiring our obedience on this issue today!

The Three Roof Coverings (Exodus 26:7-14)

Above the ten curtains of finely twisted linen that were interwoven with blue, purple, and scarlet yarn and imprinted with cherubim were the three coverings that formed the roof of the Holy Sanctuary. The innermost covering of the roof was of *pure white goat's hair;* and on top of that was the middle covering of the roof made of *ram's skins dyed red;* and above that, was the uppermost covering of the roof—a waterproof covering made of *leather hides.* All of these speak to us of Jesus, our perfect covering and protection from the storms of life.

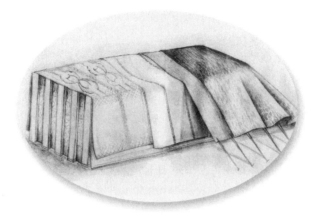

THE INNER COVERING OF GOAT'S HAIR (EXODUS 26:7-13)

Of the three coverings, the most detail is given to the innermost one—the covering of pure white goat's hair. According to Exodus 26:7 and 35:26, this covering was made of 11 panels of woven fabric, each one 45 feet long and 6 feet wide, spun from goat's hair by willing and skilled women. According to Exodus 26:11, these 11 panels were then all joined together by 50 bronze clasps, "to fasten the tent together *as a unit*" (*"that it may be one,"* KJV). The *50* clasps are a picture of the Holy Spirit's baptizing work, making us one Body; *50* is the Pentecostal number. The *bronze* speaks of God's just judgments against sin, a purifying covering in the Church. (The righteous dealing of God in the hypocrisy of Ananias and Sapphira in Acts chapter 5 is an illustration of this.)

The goat, whose hair was woven to make this covering, was used as a sin offering, significantly on the Day of Atonement (see Lev. 16:5;15-16), prefiguring our Lord Jesus Christ. "He is the atoning sacrifice for our sins, and not only for ours but also *for the sins of the whole world*" (1 John 2:2).

Finally, this covering was a *sufficient covering*. It not only covered the top of the Tabernacle, but it hung over the back and over the sides of the Tabernacle (see Exod. 26:12-13). As His Church we have a *sufficient covering*—the righteousness of Jesus Christ seen in these 11 large, pure white panels. He is the "Righteous One…the atoning sacrifice for our sins…" (1 John 2:1-2).

THE MIDDLE COVERING OF RAM'S SKINS DYED RED
(EXODUS 26:14)

As with the middle *matzoh* in the Matzoh Tosh of the Passover Seder, which we will yet discuss, this middle covering of the Tabernacle has great messianic significance. This covering of ram's skins speaks to us of Jesus, foreshadowed by the ram that Abraham offered as a substitute for his son Isaac.

> *"Abraham looked up and there in a thicket he saw a ram caught by its horns. He went over and took the ram and sacrificed it as a burnt offering instead of his son"* (Genesis 22:13).

This middle Tabernacle covering further speaks to us of Jesus, foreshadowed by the sacrifice of the two rams in the consecration of Aaron and his sons to the holy priesthood.

> *"Take one of the rams, and Aaron and his sons shall lay their hands on its head. Slaughter it and take the blood and sprinkle it against the altar on all sides. Cut the ram into pieces and wash the inner parts and the legs, putting them with the head and the other pieces. Then burn the entire ram on the altar. It is a burnt offering to the Lord, a pleasing aroma, an offering made to the Lord by fire. Take the other ram, and Aaron and his sons shall lay their hands on its head. Slaughter it, take some of its blood and put it on the lobes of the right ears of Aaron and his sons, on the thumbs of their right hands, and on the big toes of their right feet. Then sprinkle blood against the altar on all sides. And take some of the blood on the altar and some of the anointing oil and sprinkle it on Aaron and his garments and on his sons and their garments. Then he and his sons and their garments will be consecrated"* (Exodus 29:15-21).

Consequently, this covering was made of "ram's skins *dyed red*," amplifying the atonement that is ours through the blood of our Lord Jesus Christ, our sufficient covering. Looking down on the Tabernacle, God could say, *"When I see the blood, I will pass over you"* (Exod. 12:13).

The Topmost Covering of Leather Hides (Exodus 26:14)

The NIV states this was "a covering of hides of sea cows." The KJV uses the phrase "badger skins," though this is unlikely, for we are told that badgers are not native to that area. The Amplified Bible translates this phrase as "dolphin or porpoise skins," and The Message uses the phrase "dolphin skins," referring to a sea creature abundant in the waters of the Red Sea. This covering was probably not very attractive or appealing, for Jesus "…had no beauty or majesty to attract us to Him, nothing in His appearance that we should desire Him" (Isa. 53:2). And what was true of Him would always be true of His people:

> *He chose the lowly things of this world and the despised things…to nullify the things that are, so that no one may boast before Him* (1 Corinthians 1:28-29).

The only thing attractive about the Tabernacle was the glory that hovered over it; so it is with Jesus, and so it is of His true Church.

Finally, this covering was waterproof—"a refuge and hiding place from the storm and rain" (Isa. 4:6). In every sense of the word, these protective coverings speak to us of Jesus, our sufficient protective covering "from the storm and rain" of human tragedy.

The Upright Frames of Acacia Wood (Exodus 26:15-30)

Moses was told by the Lord: "Make upright frames of acacia wood for the tabernacle" (Exod. 26:15). The KJV translates "upright frames" as "boards." There were 48 of these upright boards, each one made of acacia wood overlaid with gold (see Exod. 26:18,20,25,29), a picture of the human nature covered by the divine nature—a picture of

Jesus Himself and also of what Jesus comes to do in us. On these golden upright boards were draped the linen curtains and the three top protective coverings. Each board, as it was placed upright, stood 15 feet (10 cubits) tall and was 2¼ feet (1½ cubits) wide, making the Tabernacle 45 feet long and 15 feet wide (for the two corner boards were double (see Exod. 26:22-24).

Some years ago the Lord used a most wonderful revelation about these boards in my life. I saw that each board was 1½ half cubits wide— a number *incomplete* in itself. However, when two boards were joined together, their combined width became 3 cubits, a whole and complete number, three being the number of God Himself! I saw clearly how God seeks to reveal Himself through *joined lives!* In marriage, a man and a woman are joined as one, and they thereby become a demonstration of how Jesus relates to His bride: "This is a profound mystery— but I am talking about Christ and the church" (Eph. 5:32). Also, Jesus promised:

> ...*If* **two** *of you on earth agree about anything you ask for* [the two joined as one in heart], **it will be done** *for you by My Father...* (Matthew 18:19).

And, where at least *"two...come together* in My name, there I am with them," in the very midst of them (Matt. 18:20). Our God Himself is a perfect unity of Father, Son, and Holy Spirit, and He delights in the unity of His people! In the joining together of the upright boards, it is not the wood (picturing our humanity) that touches; rather, it is the gold that is touching the gold. Our unity comes when the imparted divine nature in my life touches the imparted divine nature in your life. It is *He* who makes us one! And this is the way God creates marriages and families and friendships and the Body of Christ itself.

Exodus 26:17 further tells us that the upright boards were held together by *"two projections* set parallel to each other." The KJV translates these two projections as "two tenons." The Hebrew literally reads "two hands." The upright boards were held together by "mortise and tenon," by "tongue and groove." The "hand" in the one board reaching out to clasp the "hand" in the other board, as demonstrated in

Galatians 2:9. This is what made the upright boards one. "In [Jesus] the whole building is *joined together* ['fitly framed together,' KJV] and rises to become a holy temple in the Lord" (Eph. 2:21).

Covenant relationship in the Body of Christ is an essential in our walk with the Lord. First of all, we are in covenant with Jesus—"This cup is *the new covenant* in My blood, which is poured out for you" (Luke 22:20). He is our very life, and we are one with Him! And we are also in covenant with *others*—the board to our left and the board to our right—joined together by divine "mortise and tenon." First Samuel 18:1;3-4 describes how:

> ...*Jonathan became* **one in spirit with David**...*And Jonathan* **made a covenant with David** *because he loved him as him- self. Jonathan took off the robe he was wearing and gave it to David, along with his tunic, and even his sword, his bow and his belt.*

This beautiful covenant relationship would be reaffirmed again and again (see 1 Sam. 20:17; 23:18). And this same covenant relation- ship was true in the early church for "all the believers were *one in heart and mind.* No one claimed that any of his possessions was his own, but *they shared everything they had*" (Acts 4:32). This is true commitment, true covenant lived out in true community.

These are the lessons of the golden boards held together by mor- tise and tenon. This is the Body of Christ "fitly framed together" (Eph. 2:21 KJV)! At this juncture we must ask ourselves—"Who is the board to *my* left and who is the board to *my* right? To whom am *I* so vitally connected? To whom am *I* committed? With whom am *I* in covenant? With what band of saints am *I* joined together in Christian commu- nity?" "Now you are the body of Christ, and each one of you is a part of it" (1 Cor. 12:27).

In the Tabernacle, each board was also firmly established on two bases ("sockets," KJV) of silver, symbolizing our firm foundation on Christ's redemption. Each base, or socket of silver, was believed to weigh one talent, or a total of 264 pounds between the two bases—a very *solid foundation.* These silver bases also separated the boards from the earth beneath them, declaring that though we are *in* the world, we are not *of it;* we are separated from it (see John 17:14,16).

The whole Tabernacle was further held together by five golden crossbars, four of which passed through *external* golden rings (see Exod. 26:26-27;29). The middle crossbar, however, was apparently hidden from sight, running through *the center* of the upright boards from end to end (see Exod. 26:28). So four crossbars were *external* and *visible* and one crossbar was *internal* and *hidden.* Five is the number of grace and here we see that grace is both *visible* and *invisible,* both *external* and *hidden.* Acts 4:33 (KJV) tells us about *visible* grace—"great grace was *upon them all.*" First Peter 3:4 (KJV) then tells us of hidden grace, resting upon *"the hidden man* of the heart." Grace *upon* the Body of Christ and grace *deep within* the Body of Christ holds His Body together as one!

THE VEIL BEFORE THE HOLY OF HOLIES (EXODUS 26:31-33)

This veil was "a curtain of blue, purple and scarlet yarn and finely twisted linen, with cherubim worked into it by a skilled craftsman" (Exod. 26:31). This veil separated the Holy of Holies from the Holy Place (see Exod. 26:33). It was this veil, in the later Temple, that was "torn in two from top to bottom" when Jesus died (Matt. 27:51), and this torn veil then became a picture of Jesus' body, torn to open the way for us into God's Presence according to Hebrews 10:19-20:

> *Therefore, brothers, since we have confidence to enter the Most Holy Place by the blood of Jesus, by a new and living way opened for us **through the curtain, that is, His body.***

From the dimensions of the boards and the curtains we conclude that the Tabernacle itself was 45 feet long by 15 feet wide by 15 feet high. The Holy of Holies, the second room in this Sanctuary, was a perfect cube—15 feet long by 15 feet wide by 15 feet high. In that perfect cube was placed the Ark of the Covenant with its atonement cover, the mercy seat, adorned with the golden cherubim of glory gazing down upon it. Between the cherubim was to rest the glory cloud, the Shekinah, the radiant Presence of God Himself!

In the first room, the Holy Place, would be found three items of furniture—the golden altar of incense before the veil, the golden table of the bread of the Presence on the north side of the room, and the golden lampstand on the south side of the room (see Exod. 26:34-35). These pieces of furniture—the Ark, the incense altar, the table of the bread of the Presence, and the lampstand—are themes we will develop next.

The veil separated the Holy of Holies and the Ark of the Covenant from the Holy Place. This separating wall was made of heavenly blue, royal purple, redeeming red, and pure white, finely twisted linen, all pictures of Jesus, with the added cherubim woven into it (see Exod. 26:31).

The veil was hung on four posts of acacia wood overlaid with gold and set in four silver bases, all bearing witness to the humanity and the deity and the redemption that is in Christ Jesus. The four posts speak of the four gospels going as good news in all four directions—N, E, W, S (north, east, west, and south)—by the witnessing Church.

THE ENTRANCE TO THE HOLY PLACE (EXODUS 26:36-37)

There were three entrances, or gates, in the Tabernacle complex. The first gate was the wide multi-colored 30-foot gate bringing one into the outer court. The second gate, which we will consider now, was the entrance into the Holy Place. This gate was hung by gold hooks to *five* posts of *acacia wood overlaid with gold* (a picture of Jesus, the God-man) and set in *five bases of bronze* (see Exod. 26:37). Five is the number of grace, inviting us to enter, and bronze is the metal declaring God's righteous dealing with our sin. The third and final gate, the veil which we previously considered, was the entrance into the Holy of Holies.

So, there were three gates—one into the outer court, one into the Holy Place, and one into the Holy of Holies. All three gates faced east toward the rising sun. All three gates were made of blue and purple and scarlet yarn woven into the finely twisted linen, speaking of the beauties of our Lord Jesus and, in turn, of His Church. Only the two gates in the Sanctuary tent itself had the additional embroidered cherubim, a testimony to the presence of angels in the life and ministry of the Church as it gathers in Jesus' Name. And all three gates speak of Jesus, Himself the Gate of entrance into the courts of the Lord (see John 10:7).

One concluding thought: in Matthew 13:23 Jesus speaks of good seed, the Word of God, falling on good ground, on the hearing, understanding heart, and "yielding a hundred, sixty or thirty times what was sown." The outer courts represent that 30-fold yield; the Holy Place represents that 60-fold yield; and the Holy of Holies represents that 100-fold yield. Our God is ever calling us to go deeper and further in Him! The outer courts were illuminated by God-given natural light—the light of the sun and the moon and the stars. The Holy Place was illuminated by the anointed golden lampstand. But the light in the Holy of Holies came alone from the glory cloud, the presence of God Himself—the ultimate of all our experiences in God. And so we are being called by the Holy Spirit from the glorious *things* of God to the very glory of *God Himself!* He Himself is our hundred-fold portion.

PRAYER OF CONSECRATION

Lord of Heaven, thank You for Your Body, the Church. Thank You for making us all one in Yourself. Thank You for committed, covenant relationship in Your House. I do give myself to You to be "built together," to be "knit together" into Your holy temple. I thank You that You are our sufficient covering. I thank You for Your blood and righteousness. And I thank You for Your call to come closer, to walk deeper with You. Lord, bring me into the Holy of Holies; bring me in by the blood of the Lamb! In Your precious Name. Amen!

Chapter 4

THE HOLY PLACE—
THE GOLDEN LAMPSTAND

(Exodus 25:31-39; 27:20-21; 37:17-24)

THE golden lampstand is spoken of 30 times in Holy Scripture. The KJV word "candlestick" is not an accurate translation of the Hebrew word *menorah*, as candles and candlesticks only appeared in the Roman era much later in time. *Menorah* is correctly translated "lampstand." Twenty-one times (7 × 3) in the Gospels Jesus Himself is called "the Light," but in Matthew 5:14, He declares of His followers, *"You are the light* of the world…."* Revelation 1:20 consequently interprets "the seven lampstands" of Revelation as "the seven churches." So the menorah, the golden lampstand, becomes for us a beautiful picture of both Christ and His Church: the light of the world!

The Value of the Lampstand

In Exodus 25:39-40 Moses was instructed by the Lord: *"A talent of pure gold* is to be used for the lampstand and all these accessories. See that you make them according to the pattern shown you on the mountain."* A talent of gold weighs about 75 pounds, or 1,200 ounces. At the present price of gold, we are speaking here of a value of over $1,000,000! Also, 75 pounds of gold made a rather large and impressive lampstand!

The Function of the Lampstand

The lampstand stood on the south side of the Holy Place, to the left as one entered the door. And the command was given, "Make its seven lamps and set them up on it *so that they light the space in front of it"* (Exod. 25:37). The lampstand with its seven lamps shed light on the golden table of the bread of God's Presence and also on the golden altar of incense before the veil. The lampstand also illuminated the golden boards, mortised together to form the walls of the golden Sanctuary. And the lampstand also illuminated the beautiful white curtains with the embroidered cherubim, which formed the ceiling of the Sanctuary. All of the beauty of the Sanctuary was revealed in the light that shone from the golden lampstand. And so it is with the anointing of the Holy Spirit, which Jesus carries and which is now poured out upon His Church. That anointing brings to light all the perfections and graces found in our Lord Jesus Christ and in His Church!

The Beauty of the Lampstand

The Lord instructed Moses, "Make a lampstand of pure gold and hammer it out, base and shaft..." (Exod. 25:31). *Pure gold* speaks of the undefiled divine nature of our Lord Jesus Christ, "...who is holy, blameless, pure, set apart from sinners, exalted above the heavens" (Heb. 7:26). And it is that divine nature that *we* also partake of as His Church (see 2 Pet. 1:4)!

"*Hammer* it out," Moses was told. The KJV translates that expression, "of *beaten* work shall the candlestick be made" (see Exod. 25:31). We are reminded of the pathway our Savior walked, to which He now invites us as we "follow in His steps" (1 Pet. 2:21)—a pathway of suffering. "I offered My back to those who *beat Me...*" (Isa. 50:6)—"of *beaten* work shall the candlestick be made"! "...We considered Him *stricken by God, smitten* by Him, and *afflicted*" (Isa. 53:4). Of *beaten* work shall the candlestick be made. Precious Lord Jesus!

"...Its flowerlike cups, buds and blossoms *shall be of one piece with it*" (Exod. 25:31). The word *integrity* means "to be one complete, undivided whole." This lampstand with all of its decorative work—speaking of Christ and His Church—is a demonstration of *integrity; it is one complete, undivided whole.* Here we see the integrity of Christ and the integrity of His Church!

THE SIX BRANCHES OF THE LAMPSTAND

Exodus 25:32 is enlightening to us: "Six branches are to extend from the sides of the lampstand—three on one side and three on the other." The lampstand, strictly speaking, is that one central, decorated, golden *shaft* that rests on the golden *base*: "Make a lampstand of pure gold... *base and shaft...*" (Exod. 25:31). We are now told that an additional six branches are to *extend out from the sides of this lampstand.* The KJV, as the Hebrew text, states that the six branches are to "*come out of the sides*" of the lampstand—just as Eve was "*taken out* of the man's side" (Gen. 2:22-23, Hebrew). The six branches speak of the Church, Christ's Bride, brought forth out of His wounded side.

Six is the human number, the number of incompleteness. The Church in its humanity is incomplete in itself, but when joined to Christ, the Church becomes "complete in Him," signified by the number seven. Paul glories in this truth that in Christ "...dwells all the fullness of the Godhead bodily; and *[we] are complete in Him* who is *the head of all...*" (Col. 2:9-10 NKJV). As "Head of all," our Lord is *exalted above all.* As we shall shortly see, the central lampstand is placed *higher* than the six other branches that come out from it, demonstrating the centrality and supremacy of our Lord Jesus Christ.

THE ALMOND DECORATIONS

Focusing on these six branches that come out of the lampstand, Moses is told:

> *Three cups shaped like **almond flowers with buds and blossoms** are to be on one branch, three on the next branch, and the same for all six branches extending from the lampstand* (Exodus 25:33).

Three is the number of God Himself and *almond flowers and buds and blossoms* speak of resurrection life. The almond tree blossoms before any other tree, as spring is birthed out of winter. And the budding almond tree speaks of the resurrection life of our Lord Jesus Christ within His Church. And so the Church, as Jesus Himself, bursts with resurrection life!

When Aaron was challenged by those who opposed his leadership, it was the Lord Himself who bore witness to Aaron's ministry, for Aaron's rod "not only sprouted but had budded, blossomed and produced almonds" (Num. 17:8)—the testimony of resurrection life!

Over the years that I have served the Lord, I have seen folks rise up from time to time—often without cause and sometimes with seeming cause—to oppose not only my leadership but also the leadership of other servants of God. I sense opposition to leadership is "par for the course." But I have also seen how the manifest blessing of God upon the ministry of His anointed servants has evidenced His choice of them, while the opposition has just diminished and dissipated. Above and beyond anything we could ever do or say to validate ourselves or our ministries—beyond all else—we need a demonstration of the resurrection life of Jesus in and through us. When the almond rod produces buds and blossoms and almonds, the issue is clearly settled!

Jesus: Higher Than Any Other

The central shaft, the lampstand itself, now comes into focus: "And on the lampstand there are to be *four* cups shaped like almond flowers with buds and blossoms." And *in addition* to this fourth set of decorations:

> *One bud shall be under the first pair of branches extending from the lampstand, a second bud under the second pair, and a third bud under the third pair—six branches in all* (Exodus 25:34-35).

The six branches each had *three* sets of decorative almond work, but the central shaft, the lampstand, had *four,* and in addition to this fourth set three extra almond "buds" were fashioned at the three places from which each of the three sets of branches extended from the lampstand.

Taken all together, these extra almond decorations caused the lampstand, the central shaft, to stand *higher than any other.* The resurrection life coursing through our Lord Jesus Christ—"I am the Living One; I was dead, and behold I am alive for ever and ever!" (Rev. 1:18)—exalts Him "far above all." Paul writes of Jesus, "He is *the head* of the body, the church...*the firstborn from the dead; that in all things He might have the preeminence*" (Col. 1:18 KJV). The NIV translates that last phrase: "so that *in everything He might have the supremacy.*" This is clearly seen in the golden lampstand and its additional six golden branches. Hallelujah!

Exodus 25:36 captures our thoughts—"The buds and branches shall *all be of one piece with the lampstand, hammered out of pure gold.*" The union of Christ with His Church and the unity of the Church itself come out of the redemptive sufferings of the great God-Man, *"of one piece with the lampstand, hammered out of pure gold."*

The Seven Lamps

The "seven lamps" spoken of in Exodus 25:37, one sitting on the top of each of the six branches and one on the top of the middle lampstand, speak to us of the fullness of the seven-fold Holy Spirit of God. The Holy Spirit first anointed our great High Priest, Jesus, and now flows down to the remotest members of His Body (see Ps. 133:2). We are told in Revelation 4:5 that "…Before the throne, seven lamps were blazing. *These are the seven spirits* [margin: 'the sevenfold Spirit'] *of God.*" Our understanding of this "sevenfold Spirit" is drawn from that amazing messianic prophecy found in Isaiah 11:1-2:

> *A shoot will come up from the stump of Jesse; from his roots a Branch will bear fruit. The **Spirit of the Lord** will rest on Him—the **Spirit of wisdom and of understanding**, the **Spirit of counsel and of power**, the **Spirit of knowledge and of the fear of the Lord**.*

This seven-fold anointing rests upon our living Head and is now distributed to each of the members of His Body—the Holy Spirit in wisdom and understanding, counsel and power, knowledge and the reverence of the Lord. Amen!

The Oil for the Seven Lamps

Exodus 27:20-21 gives further instructions about the oil for these seven lamps: "Command the Israelites to bring you *clear oil of pressed olives* for the light *so that the lamps may be kept burning…keep the lamps burning before the Lord….*"

A continual flow of oil, to "keep the lamps burning," is the will of the Lord for His people. The amazing vision given to the prophet Zechariah for Zerubbabel, the temple builder, bears this out. In this vision, Zechariah saw:

> *…a solid gold lampstand with a bowl at the top and seven lights on it, with seven channels to the lights. Also there are two olive trees by it, one on the right of the bowl and the*

other on its left ["feeding it continuously with oil," AMP] (Zechariah 4:2-3).

When asked what this vision meant, the angel of the Lord said to Zechariah: "...This is the word of the Lord to Zerubbabel: 'Not by [human] might nor by [human] power, but *by My Spirit,*' says the Lord Almighty" (Zech. 4:6). All our life and all our service are to be lived in the might and in the power of the ongoing, overflowing fullness of God's Holy Spirit! *"Keep the lamps burning before the Lord...."*

"CLEAR OIL OF PRESSED OLIVES"

The KJV of Exodus 27:20 refers to "pure olive oil *beaten* for the light"; the NIV translates that as "clear oil of *pressed* olives." I have pondered the words "beaten" and "pressed." The statement when used in reference to the suffering Messiah—"hammered ['beaten,' KJV] out of pure gold" (Exod. 25:36)—is easier to understand. The Suffering Servant of Isaiah pictures the Messiah as exactly that (see Isa. 50:6; 52:14; chapter 53). But how could we refer to the unblemished Holy Spirit (typified by the pure, clear oil) as One who also has been "beaten" or "pressed"? In what way has the Holy Spirit *suffered*? Actually, the whole Godhead—Father, Son, and Holy Spirit—*suffers* at the hands of man!

Concerning the sufferings of the Holy Spirit, we see Him in Romans 8:26, praying with *"groans that words cannot express"*! J.B. Phillips translates these as *"agonizing longings."* Ephesians 4:30 also presents us with the Holy Spirit's grief: "...Do not *grieve* the Holy Spirit of God...." The Message translates these words, *"Don't break His heart."* J.B. Phillips translates them as "Never *hurt* the Holy Spirit;" The Living Bible translates them as: "Don't cause the Holy Spirit *sorrow*...." Isaiah 63:10 states that Israel *"grieved* ['*vexed,*' KJV] His Holy Spirit," and First Thessalonians 5:19 (NKJV) implies His potential hurt in the statement: "Do not *quench* ['*suppress,*' TM; 'never damp the fire,' Phillips; '*stifle,*' NEB] the Spirit." And our Lord Jesus expresses alarm at the thought of the one who *"blasphemes* against the Holy Spirit" (Mark 3:29). The

Greek word *blasphemeo* means "to speak injuriously;" the Hebrew word means "to pierce, to sting." *Webster's* defines blasphemy as "to speak evil of; to curse or revile; to speak contemptuously of; to mock."

Our triune God is a suffering God, suffering at the hands of His creation! So it was with our Lord Jesus, and so it is with His Holy Spirit. He has suffered! And that suffering, that crushing, that pain has only demonstrated all the more the purity of the Holy Spirit of God! He is the "pure olive oil *beaten* for the light...." And only through Him and His faithfulness can we *"keep the lamps burning* before the Lord" (Exod. 27:21).

TRIMMING THE LAMPS

Finally, we are presented with a necessity for the proper burning of the lamps. These instructions are given to Moses: "Its *wick trimmers* and trays are to be of pure gold" (Exod. 25:38). The trimming of the charred wicks is essential if the light would shine bright and clear. The exact same thought is presented to us in the analogy of the vine and the branches, very similar to the lampstand and its branches. "I am the vine; you are the branches" (John 15:5). And if a branch is to bear fruit and more fruit and much fruit, it must be trimmed also—pruned "so that it will be even more fruitful" (John 15:2). The primary pruning tool is His Word: "You are already clean [pruned] because of the word I have spoken to you" (John15:3). But if and when we fail to respond to His word, the faithful and constant Gardener will resort to other measures:

> *My son, do not make light of the Lord's discipline, and do not lose heart when He rebukes you, because the Lord disciplines those He loves, and He punishes* [lit., whips] *everyone He accepts as a son. Endure hardship as discipline; God is treating you as sons...* [and] *God disciplines us for our good, that we may share in His holiness...discipline...produces a harvest of righteousness and peace for those who have been trained by it* (Hebrews 12:5-7;10-11).

Even our Lord Jesus Christ, "who knew no sin…learned obedience from what He *suffered* and, once made perfect [mature, full grown], He became the source of eternal salvation for all who obey Him" (Heb. 5:8-9). And so with us. Indeed, "let your light so shine before men, that they may see your good works, and glorify your Father…in heaven" (Matt. 5:16 KJV). Amen!

PRAYER OF CONSECRATION

Heavenly Father, I thank You for the beauty of the golden lampstand. I thank You for Christ and His Church, the light of the world! I thank You for the grace of suffering; and I thank You for the affirming resurrection life of Christ in my life. I thank You for the presence and the power of Your Holy Spirit. Spirit of the Living God, fall afresh on me! Break me, melt me, mold me, fill me, use me, I pray. In Jesus' dear Name. Amen.

Chapter 5

The Holy Place—The Table of the Bread of His Presence

(Exodus 25:23-30; 37:10-16; Leviticus 24:5-9)

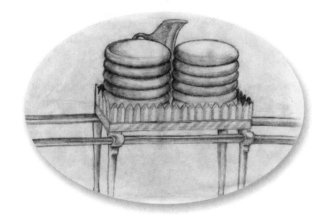

The Table of Showbread

A.B. Simpson in *Christ in the Tabernacle* calls this table "a simple little table," and this is exactly what it was.[1] Standing only 2¼ feet high, and 3 feet long, and 1½ feet wide, it was placed on the north side of the Holy Place, to the right of the door's entrance. It is mentioned in Holy Scripture 21 times (3 × 7, two very important numbers—three, the number of God, and seven, the number of completion).

The table was made of acacia wood, a symbol of humanity, both Jesus' and ours, and it was overlaid with pure gold, a symbol of the faultless divine nature of Jesus, the divine nature of which we now partake.

The KJV calls this table the "table of shewbread" ["showbread," NKJV]; the NIV calls it the table of "the bread of the Presence." The literal Hebrew text calls this the table of "the *bread of the faces.*" The bread was to appear before Jehovah "at all times" (Exod. 25:30).

THE DOUBLE CROWN

The table of the bread of the Presence had an unusual feature about it—a double crown.

> *Overlay* [the table] *with pure gold and make a gold molding* ["**a crown of gold**," KJV] *around it. **Also** make around it a rim a handbreadth wide and put a gold molding* ["a golden crown," KJV] **on the rim** (Exodus 25:24-25).

The table was twice crowned, reminding us of the beautiful statement concerning "Jesus...*crowned with glory and honor* because He suffered death, so that by the grace of God He might taste death for everyone" (Heb. 2:9). Jesus, "crowned with glory *and* honor," the double crown!

THE RIM A HANDBREADTH WIDE

The first "crown" went around the top of the table itself; the second "crown" was on top of a 3-inch rim, "a rim a handbreadth wide," that also went around the table. The "rim" was a 3-inch ledge for the purpose of keeping the 12 loaves from falling off the table, especially in journey. The bread, as we shall shortly see, speaks of Jesus, *"the living bread that came down from heaven"* (John 6:51). The 3-inch rim assures us that we shall not lose Him! Paul writes:

> *I am convinced that neither death nor life, neither angels nor demons, neither the present nor the future, nor any powers, neither height nor depth, nor anything else in all creation,*

will be able to separate us from the love of God that is in Christ Jesus our Lord (Romans 8:38-39).

But, the 12 loaves of bread also speak of the people of God, and in this case, the 12 tribes of Israel, as the number *12* indicates. And there is a special promise in the 3-inch rim that is also given to God's people, assuring us that *He will not lose us:*

> *To Him who is able to* **keep you from falling** *and* **to present you before His glorious presence** *without fault and with great joy—to the only God our Savior be glory, majesty, power and authority, through Jesus Christ our Lord, before all ages, now and forevermore! Amen* (Jude 24-25).

Even as the 3-inch rim kept the bread from falling off the table, so our God promises to *"keep us from falling"* and *"to present [us] before His glorious presence without fault* and with great joy...." The bread of the Presence was to be "before [God] at all times." "So we are presented before His glorious presence" at all times!

The Poles for Carrying the Table

We are with Him and He is with us throughout our whole journey. "I am with you *always,* to the very end of the age" (Matt. 28:20). The poles show us this promise of God's abiding Presence and provision. Made of acacia wood (humanity) overlaid with gold (the divine nature), the poles (or "staves," KJV) were for the purpose of "carrying the table" through the wilderness into the land of Promise, wherever the people of God would go! (See Exodus 25:26-28.) Jesus, our sustenance, ever with us!

"Pitchers...For the Pouring Out of Offerings"

The NIV, as well as the NKJV, translates the Hebrew correctly in Exodus 25:29: "And make its plates and dishes of pure gold, as well as its *pitchers* and bowls *for the pouring out of offerings."* We are introduced to this poured-out "drink offering" in the ordination ceremony of the priests—"a quarter of a hin [one quart] of wine as a drink offering" (Exod. 29:40), to be poured out on the altar of bronze as a sacrifice to Jehovah.

The final letter from Paul's pen was his second letter to Timothy, his spiritual son, written by Paul just before his execution. In Second Timothy 4:6, Paul writes: "I am already being *poured out like a drink offering*, and the time has come for my departure." The drink offering speaks of *an outpoured life, utterly expended* for the glory of God! This is the testimony of Jesus and also of His Church—the testimony of an outpoured life. An abandoned life. An utterly given life. And the drink offering had its place on the table of the bread of the Presence along with the bread.

"THE BREAD OF THE PRESENCE" (EXODUS 25:30)

Leviticus 24:5-9 speaks of the bread itself in these words—"Take *fine* flour and bake twelve loaves of bread" (v.5). The grain from which the flour is made comes *from the earth*—the earth that was *cursed* because of our sin (see Gen. 3:17-18). And so, our Lord Jesus, "born of a woman, born under the law," became *"a curse for us"* (Gal. 4:4; 3:13) in order to redeem us from the curse. The grain from which the flour is made also *comes out of death*, for only *"...if it dies, it produces many seeds"* (John 12:24). And then the grain becomes flour only by *grinding and crushing*, for this was to be "fine [not coarse] flour" (Lev. 24:5). Isaiah 53:5 tells us "He was *crushed* for our iniquities...." O, the beauty of the refined nature of Him who "learned obedience from what He *suffered*" (Heb. 5:8).

Finally, it takes *the fiery oven* to change the flour into bread; and so with our Lord Jesus, who for us bore the fire of God "...in the furnace of affliction" (Isa. 48:10). This is God's process for making bread. And this is the biography of Jesus, the living Bread that came down from Heaven. This is also our story, if we would be "broken bread and poured out wine" for His Church and for a lost world!

Each loaf, according to Leviticus 24:5, was made of ²/₁₀ of an ephah of flour, about 4 quarts or *6 pounds of fine flour.* These were hefty loaves! This was substantial bread. This is our sufficient Savior. This is our true nourishment!

"Pure Incense...To Represent the Bread"

Leviticus 24:6-7 further tells us:

> Set [the loaves] in two rows, six in each row, on the table of pure gold before the Lord. **Along each row put some pure incense as a memorial portion to represent the bread** and to be an offering made to the Lord by fire.

The pure incense put along the two rows of bread was to "represent the bread." This speaks to us of the high priestly intercession of our Lord Jesus as He represents us before the Father. "For Christ did not enter a man-made sanctuary that was only a copy of the true one; He entered heaven itself, *now to appear for us in God's presence*" (Heb. 9:24), where *"He always lives to intercede for [us]"* (Heb. 7:25).

"Sabbath After Sabbath"

> *This bread is to be set out before the Lord regularly, Sabbath after Sabbath, on behalf of the Israelites, as a lasting covenant.* **It belongs to Aaron and his sons, who are to eat it in a holy place,** because it is a most holy part of their regular share of the offerings made to the Lord by fire (Leviticus 24:8-9).

Week by week, Sabbath after Sabbath, new loaves were to be put out on the table, and the old loaves were to become a part of a holy "communion service" celebrated by Aaron and his sons around that simple table that hosted both the bread and the wine. (Remember not only the loaves of bread, but the drink offering, a quart of wine, was also on the table.) Week by week this celebration was held, reminiscent of the past when the priestly "Melchizedek king of Salem brought out bread and wine" to bless Abraham (Gen. 14:18-19). And all of this now points to those sons of God who today "hear His holy Word, gather 'round the table of the Lord, eat His body, drink His blood, and they'll sing a song of love..." (from a Jesus People song). It is recorded of the early believers: "On the first day of the week *we came together to break bread...*" (Acts 20:7).

Jesus told us, "I am the bread of life...whoever *eats My flesh and drinks My blood* has eternal life, and I will raise him up at the last day..." (John 6:48,54). Paul celebrates these thoughts in his rhetorical questions—"Is not the cup of thanksgiving for which we give thanks *a participation in the blood of Christ?* And is not the bread that we break *a participation in the body of Christ?*" (1 Cor. 10:16). The answers are obvious, for our Lord Jesus has declared over the bread:

> **This is My body,** which is for you; do this in remembrance of Me...[And] this cup **is the new covenant in My blood;** do this, whenever you drink it, in remembrance of Me (1 Corinthians 11:24-25).

Upon hearing these very words of Jesus, the theologians of His day immediately began to argue among themselves: *"How can this man give us His flesh to eat?"* (John 6:52). And the theologians of today still argue that point! Transubstantiation?[2] Consubstantiation?[3] Symbols or realities? But above the debate, all Jesus does is simply reiterate His point: "Unless you *eat the flesh of the Son of Man* and *drink His blood,* you have no life in you" (John 6:53). Let's just say the "how" is a mystery, but the reality is true! "This *is* My body...this *is* the new covenant in My blood." Amen!

The Tabernacle bread speaks of Jesus Himself. He is the "Living Bread" (John 6:51), which we as a royal priesthood eat. But the 12 loaves also represent the people of God, appearing always before the Lord, as the *12* loaves imply. In the Hebrew text the bread is called "the bread of the faces," for the faces of the people of God appear continually before God in His Presence, represented by the 12 loaves on the table of the Bread of His Presence.

Paul probably had this very thought in mind when he further wrote to the Corinthians, *"We* being many *are one bread,* and one body: for we are all partakers of that one bread" (1 Cor. 10:17 KJV). By eating of Jesus, we become what we eat! As we partake in faith of the one bread, *we become* that one bread! As we eat His body, *we become* His Body! "We…are *one bread,* and *one body; for we are all partakers of that one bread."* Praise God!

And so we see something of the beauty of the table of the bread of His Presence and the mystery of the 12 loaves set out before the Lord—beautiful pictures of Christ and His Church!

PRAYER OF CONSECRATION

Lord Jesus, thank You for that simple little table that You have prepared for me in the presence of my enemies. Thank You that my cup of blessing runs over. Thank You that the bread of Your Presence is sufficient food! I bless You! And in faith I *do* receive *You* as my spiritual nourishment, as my food and my drink. I eat of You, by faith, in the Spirit, this very day! Thank You. In Your dear Name. Amen.

ENDNOTES

1. A.B. Simpson, *Christ in the Tabernacle* (Camp Hill, PA: Christian Publications, 1987), p. 63.

2. Transubstantiation: The Catholic view that in the Eucharist, the essential substance of the bread and of the wine are *changed into* the body and blood of Christ.

3. Consubstantiation: The Reformation view that in the Eucharist the body and blood of Christ are *present with* the bread and the wine, without changing their essential substance.

Chapter 6

The Holy Place—
The Golden Altar of Incense

(Exodus 30:1-10; 30:34-38; 30:22-33; 37:25-29)

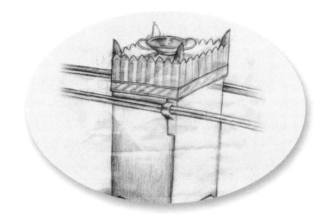

Adoration and Intercession

THE altar of incense, made of acacia wood (a symbol of the human nature) and overlaid with pure gold (a symbol of the divine nature), is a picture of our Lord Jesus Christ, the God-Man, in His role as our great intercessor. "He always lives *to intercede for [the saints]*" (Heb. 7:25). The golden altar is also a picture of the holy priesthood that Jesus has raised up in its role of adoration and intercession. The rising smoke of the burning incense is a symbol of both the praises and the prayers of this holy priesthood. Revelation 5:8 paints this very picture for us. The heavenly attendants "each...had a harp [for praise] and they were holding *golden bowls full of incense, which are the prayers of the saints.*" This is the heavenly "harp and bowl" ministry of adoration and intercession.

The psalmist David, seeing *himself* as an altar of incense, had declared, "May *my prayer be set before You like incense;* may *the lifting up of my hands* [in adoration and praise] be like the evening sacrifice" (Ps. 141:2). The KJV of Exodus 30:7 states of the altar that Aaron "shall burn thereon *sweet* incense," and in Second Samuel 23:1 (KJV), David, himself, is called "the *sweet* psalmist of Israel," thus tying these thoughts together for us.

Revelation 8:3-4 adds to this inspiring picture a slightly different thought. Here the incense, which we believe to be *the intercessions of Christ,* is added to the prayers of the saints:

> *Another angel, who had a golden censer, came and stood at the altar. He was given* **much incense to offer, with the prayers of all the saints,** *on the golden altar before the throne. The smoke of* **the incense, together with the prayers of the saints,** *went up before God from the angel's hand.*

HIGHER THAN THE OTHER FURNITURE

In Exodus 30:2 we are told that this altar "is to be square, a cubit [1½ feet] long and a cubit [1½ feet] wide, and the two cubits [3 feet] high. From these dimensions we learn that this golden altar was *higher* than the other furnishings in the Sanctuary, underscoring its importance. A.B. Simpson observes, "Prayer is the greatest of the ministries. It is much greater than preaching. It is the best thing we can do for God"[1] I personally expect that when I stand before the Lord in that great Day, I will not regret not preaching more, but I will deeply regret not praying more, not worshiping more.

THE SACRIFICE OF PRAISE

An interesting statement then follows in Exodus 30:2: *"Its horns [are] of one piece with it."* Since this is not an altar of animal sacrifice such as the bronze altar in the outer court, we are caused to wonder why it should have "horns." Psalm 118:27 (NKJV) explains the function of the "horns": "Bind the sacrifice with cords...to *the horns* of the altar." The cords were tied first to the horns of the bronze altar and were then cast over the sacrifices on the altar, securing the sacrifices, preventing them from falling off the altar. But why would the golden altar of incense need "horns," especially in view of the prohibition, "Do not offer on this altar...any burnt offering..." (Exod. 30:9)? This was clearly not an altar for animal sacrifice.

Hebrews 13:15 sheds light on this for us: "Through Jesus, therefore, let us continually offer to God *a sacrifice of praise*—the fruit of lips that confess His name." This *was* an altar of sacrifice—one of *praise,* the fruit of our lips that confess His Name! Prayer and praise become sacrifices when they cost us something. In times when we do not feel like praying, when we are not inclined to praise, and still we intercede and adore in spite of our feelings and our inclinations, then they become costly sacrifices, heaped up and tied by the Spirit to the horns of the altar!

THE GOLDEN CROWN

Exodus 30:3 continues: "Overlay the top and all the sides and the horns with pure gold [the spotless divine nature], and make *a gold molding* ["*crown,*" KJV] *around it.*" This altar was royally "*crowned,*" for this is the ministry of a "*royal* priesthood" (see 1 Pet. 2:9). This is the altar of our King, Jesus, and the altar of His priestly, kingly sons. The practical purpose for the *crown* was to keep the incense from falling off when the altar was moved, for as with Jesus, nothing is to move us from our secret place of prayer and adoration.

A GIANT CENSER

The next requirement is intriguing:

> Make **two gold rings** for the altar below the molding—two on opposite sides ["by the two corners," KJV]—to hold the poles used to carry it. Make the poles of acacia wood and overlay them with the gold (Exodus 30:4-5).

The other mobile pieces of furniture had *four golden rings* (see Exod. 25:12,26; 27:4) for the two carrying staves. Each stave, or pole, would pass through *two rings* on each side of the respective pieces of furniture enabling it to be transported with unswerving stability. The altar of incense, however, had only *two golden rings,* each attached to the two opposite corners of the altar through which each of the two staves passed respectively. This enabled the altar of incense to *swing* back and forth while it was in transit. The whole altar thus became *a giant censer,* swaying back and forth in travel!

As I have watched devout Jews swaying back and forth at the Wailing Wall in Jerusalem and as I have watched Spirit-anointed choirs swaying from side to side as they sing and as I have watched devout believers rock back and forth in fervent intercession, I have thought to myself, these are *living censers of holy incense before the Lord.* They are God's golden altar of incense! So the Lord has promised that in these last days:

> "My name will be great among the nations, from the rising to the setting of the sun. **In every place** incense and pure offerings will be brought to My name, because My name will be great among the nations," says the Lord Almighty (Malachi 1:11).

What wonderful days these are on the face of the earth as the Lord is raising up an altar of incense "in every place"—filling the air with joyful adoration and fervent prayer!

THE PLACE OF THE GOLDEN ALTAR

In Exodus 30:6 Moses is told:

> *Put the altar **in front of the curtain** that is **before** the ark of the Testimony—before the atonement cover ["the mercy seat," KJV] that is over the Testimony—where I will meet with you.*

Clearly the golden altar of incense was to be in the Holy Place, before the veil, just outside of the Holy of Holies. Hebrews 9:2-5, however, places the golden altar of incense *in the Holy of Holies:*

> *A tabernacle was set up. In its first room were the lampstand, the table and the consecrated bread; this was called the Holy Place. Behind the second curtain was a room called the Most Holy Place [the Holy of Holies], **which had the golden altar of incense** and the gold-covered ark of the covenant....Above the ark were the cherubim of the Glory, overshadowing the atonement cover....*

In Exodus 30 we are told that the golden incense altar was *in the Holy Place.* But in Hebrews 9 we are told that it was *in the Most Holy Place, the Holy of Holies!* Several explanations exist, but underscoring them both is the truth that intercession and adoration *are Holy of Holies functions!* They are our two highest callings!

The golden altar of incense belongs *in* the Holy of Holies once a year, on the Day of Atonement—the only time any man presented himself before God in the Holy of Holies—on that day the golden censer of the altar of incense went into the Holy of Holies. On the Day of Atonement Aaron was told:

> *Take a censer full of burning coals from the altar before the Lord and two handfuls of finely ground fragrant incense and take them **behind the curtain**...and the smoke of the incense will conceal the atonement cover ["the mercy seat"] above the Testimony, so that [he] will not die (Leviticus 16:12-13).*

No one could gaze upon the unveiled glory of God revealed between the cherubim and live; and no one could look upon the "awe-ful" place of atonement, the "mercy seat," and live. Consequently, on the Day of Atonement billowing clouds of incense filled the Holy of Holies with a dense smoke, making it impossible for Aaron to see anything clearly. In this way the golden altar of incense was to be found in the Holy of Holies, at least once a year!

Another explanation for the seeming contradiction as to where exactly the altar of incense was to be placed—shared with me by one of the sisters in our congregation—is that Hebrews 9:2-4 had been written decades *after* the separating veil was torn from top to bottom by God on that awesome day on which Jesus was offered up for the sins of the world. And so when Hebrews 9:24 was written, the true altar of incense was to be found in the immediate presence of the Ark, with no veil to separate it from the Holy of Holies. The golden altar of incense was thus a part of the heavenly Holy of Holies, the Most Holy Place!

REGULATIONS FOR THE GOLDEN ALTAR

"Aaron must *burn* fragrant incense on the altar *every morning* [and]...again...*at twilight so incense will burn regularly before the Lord...*" (Exod. 30:7-8). Aaron was commanded to "*burn* fragrant incense...." It was *the fire* that released the fragrance of the incense. Most certainly, it is the fire of the Holy Spirit in our lives that releases intercession and adoration. That is why we are admonished to be ever filled with the Spirit and to "*pray in the Spirit*" (Eph. 5:18; 6:18; Jude 20).

But fire can represent more; it can speak of suffering, that fiery trial that brings an amazing grace with it into our lives, releasing previously unknown depths of intercession and adoration before the Lord. I have found this to be so true in my own walk with our Lord. Peter speaks in First Peter 1:6-7 of the refining fire that *results* in "praise, glory and honor," and the author of Hebrews connects the sufferings of Jesus

Himself with His priestly ministry of intercession before the Father (see Heb. 2:18; 5:7-10).

The incense was to be burned "every morning" and "at twilight" so "incense [would] burn *regularly before the Lord* for the generations to come" (Exod. 30:7-8). This speaks to us of *continual* prayer and *continual* praise. That is why we are admonished to *"pray continually"* (1 Thess. 5:17); and also "let us *continually* offer to God a sacrifice of *praise..."* (Heb. 13:15).

No *"other"* incense was to be offered on the golden altar. The KJV translates this as "no *strange* incense." True adoration and true intercessions are to be born of the Holy Spirit and not born out of human sentiment or emotionalism.

> *Once a year Aaron shall make **atonement** on its horns. This **annual atonement** must be made with the blood of the atoning sin offering for the generations to come. It is most holy [a "holy of holies"] to the Lord* (Exodus 30:10).

Apparently, on the Day of Atonement the golden altar of incense *itself* needed to be cleansed, because nothing can enter His holy Presence uncleansed. This tells us that our prayers and praises are efficacious only through Jesus' atoning blood! Blood from the sin offering was taken from the altar of bronze in the outer courts and placed on the four horns of the golden altar in the Holy Place, thus connecting the intercessions within the veil to the atonement made on the bronze altar in the outer court. This same connection is made for us in First John 2:1-2 between the efficacious intercessions of our advocate, our Lord Jesus Christ, on our behalf before the Father and His "atoning sacrifice for our sins, and not only for ours but also for the sins of the whole world."

THE PRIESTLY BLESSING

Leviticus 9:23-24 paints a powerful picture for us. We are told that when Moses and Aaron came out of the Tent of Meeting, "they *blessed the people."* Verse 22 also tells us that "Aaron lifted his hands toward the people and *blessed them."* When the blessing was spoken over the people, "The glory of the Lord appeared to all the people. Fire came out from the presence of the Lord....And when all the people saw it, they shouted for joy and fell facedown." The blessing precipitated the appearing of the Glory of the Lord, and the blessing released the fire of God from Heaven! I sense the blessing is a key to the release of the revival Presence of God!

Numbers 6:22-27 gives us specific insight into the blessing that was spoken. Moses was told:

> *Tell Aaron and his sons, "This is how you are to bless the Israelites. Say to them: 'The Lord* [Yahweh/Jehovah] *bless you and keep you; the Lord make **His face shine upon you** and be gracious to you; the Lord **turn His face toward you** and give you peace.'" So they will put My name on the Israelites, and I will bless them.*

As a pastor, how I love to make these declarations over the saints in our congregation! We note that these were *not prayers;* these were *not requests* for God to act; these were *prophetic declarations;* these were *creative words* spoken by Aaron and his sons over the people of God! And above all else, at the very heart of God's blessing on His people, Aaron and his sons declared that *the face of God* would shine upon His people; they decreed that *the face of God* would be turned toward His people.

David and the other psalmists knew the importance of seeing the face of God in times of trouble. "Many are asking, 'Who can show us any good?' Let the light of *Your face shine upon us,* O Lord" (Ps. 4:6). "Let *Your face shine on Your servant;* save me in Your unfailing love" (Ps. 31:16). "May God be gracious to us and bless us and make His *face shine upon us,* that Your ways may be known on earth, Your salvation among all nations" (Ps. 67:1-2). "Restore us, O God; make *Your face shine upon us,* that we may be saved" (Ps. 80:3,7,19). No wonder David testified, "My heart says of You, *'Seek His face!' Your face, Lord, I will seek"* (Ps. 27:8). The face of God is our only light in the night shades of trouble. And the face of God is the essence of the revival Presence of God in our lives!

THE HOLY ANOINTING OIL

Exodus chapter 30 contains two concluding holy prescriptions—one for the holy anointing oil and the other for the holy incense to burn on the golden altar of incense (see Exod. 30:22-38). Let us briefly look at each of these in conclusion.

Five is the number of grace and there are five holy ingredients for making the holy anointing oil. First of all, there were "500 shekels [12½ pounds] of liquid myrrh." The Hebrew word for *liquid* is "freely flowing," for myrrh comes from *the sap* of the balsam bush. Second, there were "250 shekels [6¼ pounds] of fragrant cinnamon," ground from the inner bark of the laurel. Third, there were "250 shekels [6¼ pounds] of fragrant cane." The KJV notes this as "calamus"—sweet calamus from the pith or root of a local reed. Fourth, there were "500 shekels [12½ pounds] of cassia," made from the dried flowers of the cinnamon tree. And finally there was a "hin [4 quarts] of olive oil," pressed from the berries of the olive tree (see Exod. 30:22-24).

These were all put together in a *"compound"* (KJV), "a fragrant *blend"* (Exod. 30:25). God's holy anointing always involves a crushing, a pulverizing, a compounding of God's graces, so that something beautiful and powerful will emerge out of that brokenness—a "holy anointing oil"! The Lord commanded:

> *Use it to anoint the Tent of Meeting, the ark of the Testimony, the table and all its articles, the lampstand and its accessories, the altar of incense, the altar of burnt offering and all its utensils, and the basin with its stand. You shall consecrate them so they will be most holy, and whatever touches them will be holy* (Exodus 30:26-29).

Nothing in God's house and nothing in God's service was ever intended to function without the holy anointing oil! I heard a man of

God once state that if the Holy Spirit were suddenly taken off the face of the earth, 95% of all Christian activity would continue on just as it had before! That is a fearful thought, and I wonder how close to reality it is.

The Lord further declares, "Anoint Aaron and his sons and consecrate them so they may serve Me as priests" (Exod. 30:30). *No one* is able to serve God effectively in God's house apart from the anointing of the Holy Spirit. The anointing of the Holy Spirit must become our *daily* pursuit. Like the Ephesians, we are commanded to *"be [ever, continually] filled with the Spirit"* (Eph. 5:18; a present, passive, imperative in the Greek). May it ever be!

A very interesting statement then appears in the text of Exodus 30: "Say to the Israelites, 'This is to be My sacred anointing oil *for the generations to come'"* (30:31). It is interesting to note that, according to the measure of the ingredients, a *large* supply of anointing oil was prepared, enough to last *"for the generations to come,"* sufficient to anoint the Tabernacle and the Temple at its inception and sufficient to anoint prophets and priests and kings "for the generations to come." I recently heard someone say that the anointing oil actually lasted through the generations *until Messiah Himself came!* Now that He has come, it is *He* who baptizes "with the Holy Spirit and with fire" (Matt. 3:11; Mark 1:8; Luke 3:16; John 1:33; all four witnesses testify to this!). Thus it was that the type was swallowed up by the reality when Jesus appeared.

As a sidebar, it is also interesting to note that because of the ongoing twice-daily use of the incense, no initial measures were given to the ingredients of the incense, and consequently no statement was made that the initial batch of incense was to be "for the generations to come." The incense would be compounded again and again over the years until the type would finally be swallowed up by the reality, in the coming of the Messiah.

Of the holy oil, the command was further given: "Do not pour it on men's bodies"—the anointing was not for men's pleasure, to make them feel good, but rather it was "for Him," for His good pleasure! And also:

*Do not make any oil with the same formula. It is sacred, and
you are to consider it sacred. Whoever makes perfume like it
and whoever puts it on anyone other than a priest must be
cut off from his people* (Exodus 30:32-33).

Imitating the anointing was forbidden, as was imitating the sweet
incense (see Exod. 30:37-38). When men imitated the anointing or the
sweet incense or the sacred fire, as Nadab and Abihu did when they
offered "unauthorized ['strange,' KJV] fire before the Lord," judgment
inevitably followed. One can only wonder how much imitation anointing, imitation incense, and strange fire exist in the Body of Christ today.
May the passion in our lives be for reality, for the real thing!

THE HOLY INCENSE

Five is the biblical number of grace, and five ingredients are needed
for the holy incense.

*Then the Lord said to Moses, "Take fragrant spices—**gum
resin** [stacte, gum that drops from the Storax tree], **onycha** [from the shells of a clam abounding in the Red Sea,
ground fine for making perfume], and **galbanum** [the
yellow-brown gum of the Ferula shrub]—and **pure frank-
incense** [made from the gum of the Boswellia tree], all in
equal amounts, and make a fragrant blend of incense, the
work of a perfumer. It is to be salted ['tempered together,'
KJV] and pure and sacred"* (Exodus 30:34-35).

This fifth ingredient, salt, was called "the salt of the covenant of
your God" in Leviticus 2:13. The eating of salt together was one of the
ways covenant was celebrated in biblical times. Paul connects covenant
salt with covenant grace in his words to the Colossians: "Let your con-
versation be always full of *grace*, seasoned with *salt*, so that you may
know how to answer everyone" (Col. 4:6).

These five ingredients—gum resin, onycha, galbanum, frankin-
cense, and salt were to be *ground to powder, beaten very small* (KJV)

and placed "in front of the Testimony in the Tent of Meeting, where I will meet with you. It shall be most holy to you" (Exod. 30:36). *Beaten very small* and *ground to powder* speaks of suffering. Suffering makes some people *bitter*. But it makes others *better*—better intercessors, better worshipers! Jesus walked this pathway of suffering Himself, and He lays out this same pathway for us. Hebrews 2:18 simply declares, "He Himself *suffered*...;" but Hebrews 5:7-10 links His sufferings to His high-priestly ministry:

> *During the days of Jesus' life on earth, He offered up prayers and petitions with loud cries and tears....Although He was a son, He learned obedience from what He **suffered** and, once made perfect...was designated by God to be high priest in the order of Melchizedek.*

And so Peter reminds us, "To this *you were called,* because Christ suffered for you, leaving you *an example, that you should follow in His steps*" (1 Pet. 2:21).

The section on the holy incense closes with two restrictions—restricting imitation and restricting self-pleasing. "Do not make any incense with this formula *for yourselves;* consider it holy to the Lord. Whoever makes *any like it to enjoy its fragrance* must be cut off from his people" (Exod. 30:37-38). Adoration is reserved for the Lord alone. Man is not to receive glory for his own pleasure! Imitation and self-pleasing are forbidden. Anointed intercession and anointed adoration as a result of the Spirit's work in us is a ministry unto *Him*—alone!

The first coming of our Lord Jesus Christ started with events that centered around the altar of incense according to Luke 1:10-11—"When the time for *the burning of incense* came, all the assembled *worshipers* were *praying* outside. *Then an angel of the Lord appeared*...." The same scenario will usher in the Second Coming of our Lord Jesus—people fervently worshiping, people fervently praying, and then "the voice of the archangel..." will be heard as the "Lord Himself will come down from heaven, with a loud command" (1 Thess. 4:16). "He will appear a second time...to bring salvation to *those who are waiting for Him*" (Heb. 9:28)!

Prayer of Consecration

Dear Father, thank You for the message of the golden altar of incense! Thank You for Your call to prayer and praise. Thank You that I can be a censer of intercession and adoration before You. Thank You for this Holy of Holies ministry! Take Your graces and compound them together in my life to become acceptable supplication and acceptable worship in Your sight. I ask this in Jesus' dear Name. Amen.

Endnote

1. A.B. Simpson, *Christ in the Tabernacle* (Camp Hill, PA: Christian Publications, 1987), p. 79.

Chapter 7

The Holy Garments of
the Priesthood

(Exodus 28)

RIGHT in the midst of the description of the Tabernacle, the Lord suddenly introduces the subject of the holy priesthood in Exodus 28. The chapters preceding this, Exodus 25 through 27, highlight the Ark of the Covenant, the table of the bread of the Presence, the lampstand, the Tabernacle Sanctuary, the altar of burnt offering, and the holy courtyard. Then we leap over to chapter 30 where the Lord continues the divine focus on the altar of incense and the laver of bronze. The intermittent chapters 28 and 29 are a divine sidebar, focusing on the holy priesthood. Exodus, chapter 28 outlines the seven-fold garments of the holy priesthood, and chapter 29 walks us through the seven-fold ordination to the holy priesthood. This divine treatment of the material tells us that the priesthood is *central* to all that God is doing in His house. The house exists for the priesthood and the priesthood exists for the house.

Moses was told: "Have Aaron your brother brought to you *from among the Israelites*" (Exod. 28:1), reminding us of the statement in Hebrews 5:1: "Every high priest is selected *from among men*…." So it is with the Lord Jesus, our great High Priest, who was taken *from among us*, as *one of us*. He *"shared in [our] humanity…"* (Heb. 2:14). "He had to be *made like His brothers in every way*, in order that He might become a merciful and faithful high priest in service to God…" (Heb. 2:17). And so Aaron is clearly a picture of "Jesus, the apostle and high priest whom we confess" (Heb. 3:1).

God continues: "Have Aaron your brother brought to you from among the Israelites, along with *his sons* Nadab and Abihu, Eleazar and Ithamar, so they may serve Me as priests" (Exod. 28:1). If Aaron is a picture of Jesus, then whom do "his sons" prefigure? Clearly *we* are those sons. Hebrews 2:13 refers to the fatherhood of Jesus in these words: "Here am I, and *the children* God has given Me." Was not one of Jesus' grand prophetic names "Everlasting Father" according to Isaiah 9:6? In this marvelous Isaiah 9:6 prophecy the Messiah is called "a *child*" and then "a *son*" and then an "Everlasting *Father*," covering the whole gamut of human development! So close is Jesus to His Father that He is able to share in His holy fatherhood (see John 14:9-11). And we are consequently *His* sons.

The mention of the two sons, Nadab and Abihu, brings sorrow with it—for within a year these two sons would die in the Presence of the Lord for their irreverence in offering "strange ['unauthorized,' NIV] fire before the Lord" (Lev. 10:1 KJV). Our high calling as a *"holy priesthood"* (1 Pet. 2:5) carries an awesome responsibility with it. "Be *pure*, you who carry the vessels of the Lord" (Isa. 52:11).

The divine order was then given to Moses: "Make sacred [holy] garments for your brother Aaron, to give him *dignity* and *honor*" (Exod. 28:2). The KJV states that these garments "were for *glory* and for *beauty*." They were beautiful garments! They were glory robes! Let us now consider in detail these seven garments, these seven parts of the holy wardrobe, for they speak to us of Jesus, the High Priest whom we confess, and of our place by His side.

THE EPHOD (EXODUS 28:6-8; 39:2-5)

"Make the ephod of gold, and of blue, purple and scarlet yarn, and of finely twisted linen—the work of a skilled craftsman" (Exod. 28:6). This topmost garment was an embroidered vest. The NKJV margin calls the ephod the "ornamented vest." It was beautifully woven from "finely twisted linen," speaking of the spotless righteousness of our great High Priest. Woven into the pure white linen were strands of *blue* yarn, speaking of His heavenliness; and strands of *purple* yarn, speaking of His royal kingliness; and strands of *scarlet* yarn, speaking of His redemptive grace.

These materials, as we have already seen, were the basic components of the Tabernacle curtains. Thus the High Priest is directly connected to the house! The new feature now to be added is *the gold*—the "strands ['wires,' KJV] of gold" to be worked into the blue, purple and scarlet yarn and fine linen (see Exod. 39:3). Carefully, skillfully, these gold wires were woven into the cloth of the tunic, a picture of *the interwoven deity* of our Lord Jesus Christ, our great High Priest.

From the statement in Exodus 28:7, "It is to have two shoulder pieces attached to two of its corners, so it can be fastened," we gather that the vest was made of a front piece and a back piece, like front and back armor, attached at the shoulders to make one vest. Holding the vest to the body was a "skillfully woven waistband," made "of one piece with the ephod..." (Exod. 28:8). The KJV calls this waistband "the curious girdle;" the NKJV calls it "the intricately woven band of the ephod." One translation calls it "the embroidered belt." This beautiful sash is referred to in that great messianic passage, Isaiah 11:5: "Righteousness will be His belt and faithfulness the sash around His waist." Wonderful Jesus!

THE TWO ENGRAVED ONYX STONES (EXODUS 28:9-14; 39:6-7)

We consider these two engraved onyx stones as a separate part of the glory robes because of the prominence and the detail given to them.

> *Take two onyx stones and engrave on them the names of the sons of Israel in the order of their birth—six names on one stone and the remaining six on the other...Then mount the stones in gold filigree settings and fasten them on the shoulder pieces of the ephod as memorial stones [stones of remembrance]...Aaron is to* **bear the names on his shoulders** *as a memorial [a remembrance] before the Lord* (Exodus 28:9-12).

The onyx (Hebrew, *shoham)* was flesh or nail-colored, as its Hebrew name indicates. Josephus the historian called the shoulder stones "sard-onyxes"—with deep blood-red streaking the flesh tones, a vivid picture of the intense sufferings of our great High Priest in His bruised humanity.

Jesus, as the fulfillment of this great type, appears in the Presence of God for us, bearing our names in prayer before His Father, just as Aaron carried the names of Israel engraved on the onyx stones. Yes, "He is able to save completely [and forever] those who come to God through Him, *because He always lives to intercede for them*"! (Heb. 7:25).

> *Engrave the names of the sons of Israel on the two stones the way a gem cutter engraves a seal. Then mount the stones in gold filigree settings and* **fasten them** *on the shoulder pieces of the ephod...* (Exodus 28:11-12).

This tells us that Jesus' ministry for us is *fastened* and, therefore, *secure*. Jesus will *never* fail us; He will *never* forsake us. *"Never* will I leave you; [*no,*] *never* will I forsake you" [three negatives in Greek: *never, no, never!*] (Heb. 13:5).

THE BREASTPIECE (EXODUS 28:15-30; 29:8-21)

As we are studying the Tabernacle and the priesthood, we notice, as the verses listed above indicate, that *every* important issue is *spoken of twice.* Two is the number of double witness (see Deut. 19:15), and the repetition is for driving home the point and fixing it in our hearts.

The "breastpiece for making decisions," "the breastplate of judgment" (KJV) now comes into view. The length of the description and its detail makes this the most prominent part of the seven-fold holy wardrobe. As with the ephod, the breastpiece was made "of gold, and of blue, purple and scarlet yarn, and of finely twisted linen" (Exod. 28:1), all speaking of the precious nature and character of our Lord Jesus. The 18th century hymnist Samuel Medley writes about these heavenly garments of our Lord and of us His sons in the following:

> "O could I speak the matchless worth,
> O could I sound the glories forth
> Which in my Savior shine!
> I'd sing His perfect righteousness,
> And magnify the wondrous grace
> Which made salvation mine.
> I'd sing the precious blood He spilt,
> My ransom from the dreadful guilt
> Of sin and wrath divine;
> I'd sing His glorious holiness,
> In which all perfect, heavenly dress
> My soul shall ever shine.
> I'd sing the character He bears,
> And all the forms of love He wears,
> Exalted on His throne;

> In loftiest songs of sweetest praise,
> I would to everlasting days
> Make all His glories known.[1]

And so we see in all of this symbolism the beauty of our wonderful Savior!

The breastpiece was "square—a span [9 inches] long and a span [9 inches] wide—and folded double" (Exod. 28:16); it was a 9-inch square pouch, a pocket for holding several very important items, as we shall see.

The instruction continues:

> *Then mount four rows of precious stones on it. In the first row there shall be a ruby, a topaz and a beryl; in the second row a turquoise, a sapphire and an emerald; in the third row a jacinth, an agate and an amethyst; in the fourth row a chrysolite, an onyx and a jasper. Mount them in gold filigree settings. There are to be twelve stones, one for each of the names of the sons of Israel, each engraved like a seal with the name of one of the twelve tribes (Exodus 28:17-21).*

As with the onyx stones, and yet here individually, *each* of these 12 gemstones was inscribed with one of the names of the 12 tribes of Israel, and then mounted in a gold filigree setting onto the breastpiece.

The foursquare breastpiece was then fastened at its four corners to the ephod itself by means of four golden chains, "so that the breastpiece will not swing out from the ephod" (Exod. 28:22-28). In great detail a description is given of how this breastpiece is *secured* to the ephod by these four golden chains. By this we are assured of the *unfailing, unchanging* priestly ministry of our Lord Jesus Christ on our behalf, for:

> *Whenever Aaron enters the Holy Place, he will **bear the names of the sons of Israel over his heart** on the breast-*

*piece of decision as a **continuing memorial before the Lord*** (Exodus 28:29).

In all of this symbolism we are *assured* that:

*Because Jesus lives forever, He has a **permanent** priesthood. Therefore, He is able **to save completely** those who come to God through Him, **because He always lives to intercede for them*** (Hebrews 7:24-25).

Charitie Bancroft, in her great hymn, writes:

> "Before the throne of God above
> I have a strong and perfect plea
> A great high priest whose name is Love
> Who ever lives and pleads for me.
> My name is graven on His hands,
> My name is written on His heart.
> I know that while in heav'n He stands
> No tongue can bid me thence depart.
> Because the sinless Savior died
> My sinful soul is counted free
> For God the Just is satisfied
> To look on Him and pardon me.
> Behold Him there the risen Lamb
> My perfect, spotless righteousness
> The great unchangeable I AM
> The King of glory and of grace!
> One with Himself I cannot die
> My soul is purchased with His blood
> My life is hid with Christ on high
> With Christ, my Savior and my God."[2]

The instruction continues in Exodus 28:30:

Also put the Urim and the Thummim in the breastpiece, so they may be over Aaron's heart whenever he enters the presence of the Lord. Thus Aaron will always bear the means of making decisions for the Israelites over his heart before the Lord.

Two stones, the Urim (meaning "Lights") and the Thummim (meaning "Perfections") were put into the pocket of the breastpiece over Aaron's heart. These stones were given for *"making decisions* for the Israelites." Numbers 27:21 declares that the high priest "will *obtain decisions...by* inquiring of the Urim before the Lord." Exactly how these stones worked is not told to us. It is believed by some that when a decision was pending, the High Priest would take the two stones out of the breastpiece and hold them in his hands. If they glowed with the divine Presence, the decision was affirmative. Others believed they served as lots where one stone may have been one color and the other stone another color, and depending on which one the priest brought out of the pocket, God's decision would be known.

How exactly the Urim and Thummim worked, we do not know, but we do know that they *did* work. God spoke through them the knowledge of His will. The vital importance of these transactions is revealed in the phrase "over his heart" used three times in these several verses. Knowing and doing the will of God is of eternal consequence, for "the man who does the will of God lives forever" (1 John 2:17). And for this reason Jesus intercedes continually for us! He carries these issues concerning us on His heart continually!

The Urim and Thummim, speaking of the "Lights" and "Perfections" of our great High Priest Himself, assures us of Jesus' deep concern that we would be filled "with the knowledge of His will through all spiritual wisdom and understanding" (Col. 1:9). And so our Lord Jesus intercedes for us that we might stand complete in all the will of God!

THE BLUE ROBE OF THE EPHOD (EXODUS 28:31-35; 39:22-26)

Here are the garments of the Heavenly Man, the Lord from Heaven. That is the significance of this robe *all of blue.*

A fascinating command follows:

> *Make pomegranates of blue, purple and scarlet yarn around the hem of the robe, with gold bells between them. The gold bells and the pomegranates are to alternate around the hem of the robe. Aaron must wear it when he ministers. The sound of the bells will be heard when he enters the Holy Place before the Lord and when he comes out, so that he will not die* (Exodus 28:33-35).

Tradition tells us that especially when the high priest went into the Holy of Holies, the sound of the bells assured all who listened that he was acceptable and that his offerings were accepted before a holy God. The silence of the bells could only mean that the high priest had been smitten by God and that he died in God's Presence. For this reason with the passing of time, a rope was tied around the High Priest's foot as he went into the Holy of Holies so that if he were ever struck down by God, they could readily pull his dead body out of the forbidden chamber!

Attached to the hem of Aaron's beautiful blue robe were woven cloth pomegranates alternating with golden bells all around the bottom of the robe. The sounds of the bells were always to be heard as Aaron ministered before the Lord in the Holy Place. It is possible that the different bells sounded different notes, so a symphony of sound was heard from the Holy Place as Aaron ministered. The cloth pomegranates buffered the bells, keeping them from clashing one against the other and allowing each bell to sound its distinctive note as Aaron ministered. This speaks to us of the harmonious operation of the gifts of the Holy Spirit in the Body of Christ as the anointing given by the Father to Jesus our Living Head flows "down to the skirts of his garments" (Ps. 133:2 KJV). The buffering pomegranates were fruit, and Paul may have had this unusual arrangement of pomegranates and bells in mind when he wrote:

> *If I speak in the tongues of men and of angels* [as bells sounding in the Holy Place], *but have not love* [the fruit of the Spirit], *I am only a resounding gong or a clanging cymbal* (1 Corinthians 13:1).

As the absence of the pomegranates would cause the bells on Aaron's garments to clash one with another, so the absence of love, the fruit of the Spirit, causes the gifts of the Spirit to become not much more than discordant jangling in the house of God. "We have different gifts, according to the grace given us," but, in all our service, we are to "be devoted to one another in brotherly love…" (Rom. 12:6,10).

The Turban and Its Plate of Pure Gold
(Exodus 28:36-38;40; 39:30-31)

A turban ("mitre," KJV) and "headbands" ("bonnets," KJV), all out of fine linen, were made for Aaron and his sons. Attached to Aaron's linen turban, however, by means of a blue cord, was a plate of pure gold, engraved with the words "HOLY TO THE LORD" ("Holiness to the Lord," KJV). This plate of pure gold had an unusual intercessory purpose:

> It will be on Aaron's forehead, and **he will bear the guilt involved in the sacred gifts** ["the holy things," KJV] **the Israelites consecrate,** whatever their gifts may be. It will be on Aaron's forehead continually **so that they will be acceptable to the Lord** (Exodus 28:38).

What could be the "guilt involved in the sacred gifts—the holy things"? The sins of adultery and slander are more obvious; but the "guilt involved in the sacred gifts" is more subtle. Perhaps that secret feeling of pride when one's musical number went off well, or one's teaching was given without a hitch. Or perhaps that secret stirring of jealousy when God seemed to use someone else—these are a part of that "guilt involved in the sacred gifts," and need the mediatorial intercessions of our Lord Jesus so that we "will be acceptable to the Lord." Even though Paul could testify: "My conscience is clear," he yet confessed:

> …That does not make me innocent. It is the Lord who judges me…He will bring to light what is hidden in darkness and

will **expose the motives of men's hearts.** *At that time each will receive his praise from God* (1 Corinthians 4:4-5).

It appears as if even in our finest moments we can fall short of the glory of God! But thank God we have a great High Priest who always prays for us, that we will be always accepted before the Father! This holy golden plate is called the "sacred diadem" (the "holy crown," KJV) in Exodus 39:30. This is the ultimate, the grand culmination of our Lord's intercessory ministry on our behalf.

THE TUNIC ["COAT," KJV]
OF FINE WOVEN LINEN (EXODUS 28:39)

Exodus 28:39 mentions this long linen undershirt in just one phrase: "Weave the tunic of fine linen...." It was the garment worn closest to the skin—made of linen and never of wool. When the end-time Zadok priests:

> *...Enter the gates of the inner court, they are to wear linen clothes; they must **not wear any woolen garment** while ministering at the gates of the inner court...**they must not wear anything that makes them perspire** (Ezekiel 44:17-18).*

Because of the finished work of our Lord on Calvary, all priestly life and ministry is to come out of His Sabbath rest—never by any human sweat, but only by resting in the sufficient work of our Savior.

THE LINEN UNDERGARMENTS ["BREECHES," KJV]
(EXODUS 28:42-43)

The final item in the seven-fold priestly wardrobe is the:

> *...Linen undergarments as a covering for the body, reaching from the waist to the thigh. Aaron and his sons must wear them whenever they enter the Tent of Meeting or approach the altar to minister in the Holy Place, so that they will not incur guilt and die (Exodus 28:42-43).*

The KJV calls these linen undergarments, "linen breeches to cover their nakedness." Linen, pure and white is a picture of the righteousness that comes through our Lord Jesus Christ, a righteousness that covers all our carnal nakedness, so that we can approach the altar to minister in the Holy Place without incurring guilt and judgment. "This is to be a lasting ordinance for Aaron and his descendants" (Exod. 28:43). Taken together, these are the robes for "dignity and honor," for "glory and for beauty."

In closing, it is significant to note that shoes or sandals are not included in the holy wardrobe. More than likely the high priest walked barefooted, his feet touching the earth at all times, which speaks to us of Jesus who walked among us, fully identified with us in every way, except regarding sin: "tempted in every way just as we are—yet without sin" (Heb. 4:15). These are the beautiful garments! These are "the glory robes" for Jesus and for us, His sons!

Prayer of Consecration

Dear Lord Jesus, I praise You, great High Priest of my confession! I thank You for Your intercessions for me. I thank You that You ever live to pray for me and for all who are called by Your Name. I thank You that You ever carry us on Your heart and bear us up continually before our Father. And I do take my place by Your side, as one of Your sons. I thank You for calling me into Your holy priesthood. I embrace Your calling and I step into the priestly place You have prepared for me! In Your holy Name, Lord Jesus. Amen.

Endnotes

1. "O Could I Speak the Matchless Worth" by Samuel Medley; public domain.

2. "Before the Throne of God" by Charitie Bancroft; public domain.

Chapter 8

The Ordination to the Holy Priesthood and the Melchizedek Priesthood of Our Lord Jesus

(Exodus 29 and Leviticus 8)

HEBREWS 3:1 declares of Jesus that He is the *"High Priest* whom we confess."* That single statement encourages us to see Jesus the High Priest in Aaron the high priest—both in his garments and in his ordination to the holy priesthood. But the author of Hebrews goes further to develop a *new* understanding of Jesus' priesthood. The author writes: "God said to [Jesus]…'You are a priest forever, *in the order of Melchizedek*'" (Heb. 5:5-6). In Hebrews 7:11 we are given in question form *the reason* for this change in the priesthood:

> *If perfection could have been attained through the Levitical priesthood (for on the basis of it the law was given to the people), why was there still need for another priest to come— one in the order of Melchizedek, not in the order of Aaron?*

Obviously, the ineffectiveness of the Levitical priesthood necessitated a new priesthood. "The former regulation is set aside because *it was weak and useless* (for the law made nothing perfect), and a better hope is introduced, by which we draw near to God" (Heb. 7:18-19).

Actually Jesus, by virtue of His natural lineage, could never have become a Levitical priest. Jesus was not from the tribe of Levi but rather from the tribe of Judah, "For it is clear that our Lord descended from Judah, and in regard to that tribe Moses said nothing about priests" (Heb. 7:14). Consequently, a new and a different priesthood would be given to Jesus—the priesthood of Melchizedek.

At this juncture we need to ask two questions: *who* was this Melchizedek, and *how* did Jesus inherit His priesthood? First of all, "This Melchizedek was king of Salem [an ancient Jebusite city, later to become *Jerusalem]*…." Melchizedek was also:

> *…priest of God Most High. He met Abraham returning from the defeat of the kings and blessed him, and Abraham gave him a tenth [a tithe] of everything…. His name means "king of righteousness;" then also, "king of Salem" means "king of peace." Without father or mother, without genealogy, without beginning of days or end of life, **like the Son of God He remains a priest forever**** (Hebrews 7:1-3).

This is the mysterious Melchizedek! He was like Jesus and now Jesus is like him—a priest forever!

Second, we need to ask *how* exactly did Jesus inherit this Melchizedek priesthood? Coming from Judah, Jesus was a direct descendent of King David through His mother Mary, according to Luke's genealogy, but also through His foster-father, Joseph, according to Matthew's genealogy. King David was the one who conquered the Jebusite city of Salem, the ancient city of Melchizedek, and made it the capital of his empire, "the City of David" (1 Chron. 11:4-5). In that conquest, David not only captured the ancient city of Melchizedek, he also activated the priesthood of Melchizedek as well.

When David brought the Ark of the Covenant to the city of Jerusalem, he raised up a simple tabernacle, a Holy of Holies, on his estate and placed the Ark of the Covenant in that tabernacle, called the "tent of David." In Amos 9:11, the Lord promises in the last days to *restore David's fallen tent* and to repair its broken places and restore its ruins and build it as it used to be!

At this tent, this Holy of Holies, David, dressed in a *priestly robe and linen ephod, sacrificed* burnt offerings and fellowship offerings to the Lord and *blessed the people* in the name of the Lord (see 1 Chron. 15:27; 16:1-2). All of these—the linen priestly garments, the sacrifices, and the blessing—were priestly prerogatives. David moved in these because he *was* a priest.

Second Samuel 8:18 also states that "David's sons were royal advisers [Hebrew *'priests'*]." David made his sons priests. To his heir Solomon, David particularly gave this Melchizedek priesthood. In Psalm 110, a psalm of David, believed to be a coronation psalm for his son Solomon, David declares: "The Lord has sworn and will not change His mind: *'You are a priest forever, in the order of Melchizedek'"* (Ps. 110:4).

Down through the ages, the Levitical priests all died (as did David's descendants, including Solomon); "death prevented them from continuing in office," but then came Jesus, descendant of David, who also died but *was raised again to an endless life!*

> ...*Because Jesus **lives forever,** He has a **permanent priesthood**. Therefore He is able to save completely* [and forever] *those who come to God through Him, because He always lives to intercede for them* (Hebrews 7:23-25).

Jesus "has become a priest...on the basis of the power of an indestructible life. For it is declared: 'You are a priest *forever,* in the order of Melchizedek'" (Heb. 7:16-17). Praise God!

Unlike Aaron, *Jesus lives forever!* And unlike Aaron, Jesus:

> ...*does not need to offer sacrifices day after day, first for His own sins* [for He had none], *and then for the sins of the people. He sacrificed **for their sins once for all when He offered Himself*** (Hebrews 7:27).

On this glorious backdrop, let us now consider the elaborate ordination ceremony of Exodus 29 which brought Aaron into his holy priesthood. The Aaronic ordination ceremony has seven components to it, each one speaking volumes about Jesus and about us, His sons, who are His Kingdom of priests.

THE WASHING OF AARON AND HIS SONS

First, Moses is told by Jehovah:

> *This is what you are to do to consecrate them, so they may serve Me as priests....Bring Aaron and his sons to the entrance to the Tent of Meeting and* **wash them with water** (Exodus 29:1,4).

Hebrews 10:22 speaks of this: "Let us draw near to God with a sincere heart in full assurance of faith...*having our bodies washed with pure water.*" This washing speaks to us of our baptism into Christ, "in order that, just as Christ was raised from the dead through the glory of the Father, we too may live a new life" (Rom. 6:4). Every day thereafter, whenever Aaron and his sons came before the Lord, they were "to *wash their hands and feet*" at the bronze laver. There is *"one baptism,"* according to Ephesians 4:5; but there is also to be a *daily washing* of our soiled hands and feet—*a cleansing* by "washing with water *through the word*" (Eph. 5:26). In this regard, Jesus spoke to His disciples: "You are already *clean because of the word I have spoken to you*" (John 15:3). Daily, as we continue to look "intently into the perfect law that gives freedom," we are changed to become doers of the Word and not hearers only (James 1:23-25). And so we are blessed!

Even though Jesus, seen in the type of Aaron, had no sins of His own to wash away, He nonetheless was baptized in water simply to fulfill the righteousness prefigured by this washing of Aaron (see Matt. 3:13-15).

The Clothing of Aaron and His Sons

Second, Exodus 29:5-6 then states:

> **Take the garments and dress Aaron** *with the tunic, the robe of the ephod, the ephod itself and the breastpiece. Fasten the ephod on him by its skillfully woven waistband. Put the turban on his head and attach the sacred diadem to the turban.*

So we see Jesus Himself in the glory robes *"crowned* with glory and honor...." We also see Him "bringing many sons to glory," and so the command is given:

> *Bring* **his sons** *and* **dress them** *in tunics and put headbands on them. Then tie sashes on Aaron* **and his sons.** *The priesthood is* **theirs** *by a lasting ordinance. In this way you shall ordain Aaron* **and his sons** (Exodus 29:8-9).

Clothed in the righteousness of Jesus Christ Himself we, as sons, are able now to enter the Sanctuary of our God for service! "All of you who were *baptized into Christ* have *clothed yourselves with Christ*" (Gal. 3:27). Washed and clothed, the priesthood is ours by a lasting ordinance.

Anointed for Service

Third, Exodus 29:7 then tells us of Aaron, "Take the anointing oil and *anoint him by pouring it on his head.*" Aaron's anointing is further described for us in Psalm 133:2 as "precious oil poured on the head, running down on the beard, running down on Aaron's beard, down upon the collar of his robes."

This was fulfilled in Jesus' life at the river Jordan as the Father anointed Him when "the Holy Spirit descended on Him in bodily form like a dove" (Luke 3:22). Hebrews 1:9 celebrates this: "God, Your God, has set You above Your companions by *anointing You with the oil of joy.*" On that day God gave to Jesus "the Spirit without limit"

(John 3:34), and Jesus now shares that limitless anointing with all who come to Him—"If anyone is thirsty, let him come to Me and drink. Whoever believes in *Me,* as the Scripture has said, streams of living water will flow from within him" (John 7:37-38). And so Moses was commanded:

> *Bring* [Aaron's] *sons and dress them in tunics.* **Anoint them just as you anointed their father,** *so they may serve Me as priests. Their anointing will be to a priesthood that will continue for all generations to come* (Exodus 40:14-15).

Today, according to First Peter 2:5,9, we are that "holy priesthood," washed, clothed, anointed, and serving—"for all generations to come."

THE SACRIFICE OF THE SIN OFFERING

The fourth step in the consecration of Aaron and his sons was the sacrifice of the sin offering. "Bring the bull to the front of the Tent of Meeting, and Aaron and his sons shall *lay their hands on its head.*" (By this act, they declared: "This sacrifice is dying in my place; this is my substitute.") And so the word continues: "Slaughter [the bull] in the Lord's presence...It is a sin offering" (Exod. 29:10-14), necessary for us, though not for Jesus. Sinless, He needed no sin offering; and sinless, He *became* our sin offering.

> *Unlike the other high priests, He does not need to offer sacrifices day after day,* **first for His own sins,** *and then for the sins of the people. He sacrificed for* **their** *sins once for all when He offered* **Himself** (Hebrews 7:27).

Jesus Himself is that sin offering spoken of here in Exodus 29.

THE SACRIFICE OF THE BURNT OFFERING

Moses is then commanded:

> *Take one of the rams, and Aaron and his sons shall lay their
> hands on its head. Slaughter it and take the blood and sprin-
> kle it against the altar on all sides…then burn the entire ram
> on the altar. It is **a burnt offering to the Lord…** (Exodus
> 29:15-18).*

Jesus Himself is our whole burnt offering; and we, in turn, are
commanded in the language of Romans 12:1 "to offer [*our*] bodies as
living sacrifices, holy and pleasing to God," our reasonable act of worship. This was the fifth step in the consecration process.

THE SACRIFICE OF THE ORDINATION RAM

The sixth step in the ordination process, a more elaborate one, is
the sacrifice of the ordination ram. As with the first ram, "Aaron and
his sons shall lay their hands on its head [and] slaughter it." Then the
ritual grows pregnant with meaning: "Take some of its blood and put
it on the lobes of *the right ears* of Aaron and his sons, on the thumbs of
their right hands, and on the big toes of *their right feet*" (Exod. 29:20)—
that all their *hearing* and all their *doing* and all their *going* would be
under the protection of the precious atoning blood.

> *And take some of the blood on the altar and some of the
> anointing oil and sprinkle it on Aaron and his garments and
> on his sons and their garments. Then he and his sons and
> their garments will be consecrated (Exodus 29:21).*

Such rich symbolism—a holy priesthood sprinkled with precious
blood and sprinkled with the oil of gladness. The cross and the Spirit,
the blood and the fire declare our abundant redemption and sanctification in Christ Jesus!

Exodus 29:22-34 then brings us to a brand new aspect of the
ordination ceremony. The fat pieces of the ram of ordination, along
with unleavened bread from the bread basket, were to be first waved
before the Lord and then offered by fire *to Him* on His altar (see Exod.
29:22-25). Then the two most important pieces of the ordination ram

were to be presented before the Lord. *The breast* of the ordination ram was to be waved back and forth as a wave offering before the Lord, and the *thigh* ["the shoulder," KJV] of the ordination ram was to be lifted up as a "heave offering" (KJV) before the Lord. Then both *were to be given to Aaron and his sons as their share of the offering!*

> *Consecrate those parts of the ordination ram that belong to Aaron and his sons: the breast that was waved and the thigh* ["shoulder," KJV] *that was presented* ["the heave offering," KJV]. *This is* **always to be...for Aaron and his sons** (Exodus 29:27-28).

The Lord then directed:

> *Take the ram for the ordination and cook the meat in a sacred place. At the entrance to the Tent of Meeting,* **Aaron and his sons are to eat the meat of the ram** *and the bread that is in the basket.* **They are to eat these offerings by which atonement was made for their ordination and consecration...** (Exodus 29:31-33).

The atoning sacrifice clearly pictures our Lord Jesus Christ Himself. But two parts of the atoning sacrifice were to be eaten by the priests— the breast and the thigh ["shoulder," KJV]. The breast speaks to us of the compassion and lovingkindness of our Lord; and the thigh [shoulder] speaks to us of His strength and authority. Both qualities are now to be found in His servants as they eat these pieces. Both our Lord's compassionate mercy and the strength of His authority are to become ours as we partake, in faith, of His divine nature! (See Second Peter 1:4.)

Take Seven Days to Ordain Them

The seventh part of the ordination ceremony is contained in this command:

> *Sacrifice a bull each day as a sin offering to make atonement....* **For seven days** *make atonement for the altar and*

*consecrate it. Then the altar will be most holy, and what-
ever touches it will be holy...So will I consecrate the Tent of
Meeting and the altar and will consecrate Aaron and his sons
to serve Me as priests. Then I will dwell among the Israelites
and be their God* (Exodus 29:36-37;44-45).

Seven is the biblical number of perfection, of completion. *Seven*
days speaks to us of a *complete* and *perfect* provision: "By one sacrifice
He *has made perfect forever* those who are being made holy" (Heb.
10:14). And the grand conclusion of it all becomes simply this for us:

*Therefore, brothers, since we have confidence to enter the
Most Holy Place by the blood of Jesus...and since we have a
great priest over the house of God,* **let us draw near to God
with a sincere heart in full assurance of faith...** (Hebrews
10:19-22).

And so when Moses and Aaron had finished this elaborate ministry to the Lord in the Tent of Meeting:

*...They blessed the people; and the glory of the Lord appeared
to all the people. Fire came out from the presence of the Lord
and consumed the burnt offering and the fat portions on the
altar. And when all the people saw it, they shouted for joy
and fell facedown* (Leviticus 9:23-24).

God came to His holy habitation. He anointed His house and
empowered His royal priesthood!

PRAYER OF CONSECRATION

Heavenly Father, You have exalted Your Son Jesus as High
Priest forever. And Father, we, as His sons, now stand by
His side, sharing in His holy calling! Thank You for this
unspeakable honor! I thank You for the washing; I thank
You for the clothing; I thank You for the anointing; I thank
You for the priestly portion—the breast and the thigh—the

compassions and the strength that You provide. I *will* press into this, my holy calling, in Jesus' Name. Amen!

Chapter 9

The Most Holy Place,
The Holy of Holies—The Place
of the Ark of the Covenant

(Exodus 25:8-22; 37:1-9)

The Quest for God's Presence

EXODUS chapter 24 is an awesome but forbidding chapter. The Lord declared from Mount Sinai: "Moses *alone* is to approach the Lord; the others *must not come near.* And the people *may not come up* with him" (Exod. 24:2). This is in keeping with the prohibition that had been given concerning the holy mount:

> *Put limits for the people around the mountain and tell them, "Be careful that you do not go up to the mountain or touch the foot of it. Whoever touches the mountain shall* **surely be put to death.** *He shall* **surely be stoned or shot with arrows…** *Whether man or animal,* **he shall not be permitted to live**"… (Exodus 19:12-13).

In Exodus chapter 25, however, we turn a glorious corner. The Lord now decrees: "Have them make a sanctuary for Me, and *I will dwell among them"* (Exod. 25:8). At this juncture we need to ask ourselves, what caused God to so change His mind? Why were people *forbidden to draw near* to Him in chapter 24, but then encouraged to build a house for Him that He might *live among them* in chapter 25?

I believe the answer lies in the first mandate in Exodus 25:10: "Have them make a chest ['an ark,' KJV] of acacia wood…." The very first piece of furniture commanded for God's new house was the Ark of the Covenant. And the most important part of the Ark of the Covenant was the "atonement cover" [the "mercy seat," NKJV]. "And *there* I will meet with you, and *I will speak with you from above the mercy seat…* about everything…" (Exod. 25:22 NKJV). The picture becomes clear. The sinfulness of men in the light of the awesome holiness of God made it impossible for man to draw near to God. That is the message of Exodus chapter 24. But once a place of atonement had been established, once a place was set aside where sins could be forgiven and cleansed, then men could become God's welcomed guests. "I will *dwell among* them." I will *meet with you,* and *I will speak with you….*" The "mercy seat" changed it all!

There is an amazing statement made by Paul about Jesus in Romans 3:24-25: "Christ Jesus, whom God set forth as a propitiation [literally, a 'mercy seat'] by His blood…" (NKJV). The Greek text is clear; the NKJV margin picks it up by stating, God has set forth, He has publicly displayed, *Jesus* as the "mercy seat." In the old covenant the mercy seat was hidden from sight behind the thick veil in the Holy of Holies. In the new covenant the mercy seat is *publicly displayed, clearly set forth* for all to see—and that mercy seat where sin is atoned for, where sin is forgiven, where sin is cleansed—that mercy seat is the very person of *Jesus Himself!* The *Amplified Bible* captures these thoughts precisely:

> *…Christ Jesus, whom God put forward [before the eyes of all]* **as a mercy seat** *and propitiation by His blood [the cleansing and life-giving sacrifice of atonement and reconciliation, to be received] through faith…* (Romans 3:24-25).

Only because of Jesus our wonderful Savior can we now *"draw near to God* with a sincere heart in full assurance of faith, having our hearts sprinkled to cleanse us from a guilty conscience..." (Heb. 10:22)!

Moses was a man who hungered for the Presence of God (see Exod. 33:14-15). He longed to speak with God "face to face, as a man speaks with his friend" (Exod. 33:11). He had a passion for God's glory; he requested of God "show me Your glory" (Exod. 33:18). All of his longing and desire and passion would now be satisfied. Because of the atonement, God and man could be friends; they could speak "face to face." The glory of God would fill the house that Moses had prepared for Him, all because of the mercy seat—all because of Jesus!

The Most Holy Place

The Most Holy Place, the Holy of Holies, was a perfect cube, like the Holy City of Revelation 21:16. From studying the footprint of the Tabernacle building, we learn that the Holy of Holies itself was 15 feet by 15 feet by 15 feet, a perfect cube. The veil that shielded the Ark was of pure white linen, woven with heavenly blue, kingly purple, redemptive scarlet; a veil with cherubim embroidered into it, reminiscent of the cherubim who guarded "the way to the tree of life" in Genesis 3:24. This veil was called "the *shielding* ['covering,' KJV] curtain [which] *shielded* ['covered,' KJV] the ark of the Testimony..." (Exod. 40:3,21). It was this veil in the later Temple, which was torn by God Himself from top to bottom when Jesus cried out from the cross, "It is finished" (John 19:30; Matt. 27:50-51). The torn veil (a picture of Jesus' torn body) opened the way for us to enter the Holy of Holies:

> *Since we have confidence* **to enter the Most Holy Place** *by the blood of Jesus, by a new and living way opened for us through the curtain, that is, His body, and since we have a great High Priest over the house of God,* **let us draw near to God** *with a sincere heart in full assurance of faith, having our hearts sprinkled to cleanse us from a guilty conscience...* (Hebrews 10:19-22).

Praise God!

A.B. Simpson wrote: "This Holy of Holies has come to represent *the highest and deepest communion of the soul with God. This* inner chamber is the secret place of the Most High, where we can now enter through the blood of Jesus."

THE ARK OF THE TESTIMONY

Everything about the Ark, just like everything about the Tabernacle itself, speaks to us of our Lord Jesus Christ. He is the Ark of God's glory; He is the mercy seat; upon Him the glorious Shekinah (from the Hebrew word *to dwell*) rests.

> *The Word became flesh and made His dwelling* [tabernacled, literally] *among us. We have seen His **glory,** the glory of the One and Only, who came from the Father, full of grace and truth* (John 1:14).

The Ark of the Covenant is mentioned 180 times in Scripture, and in Joshua 3:11 it is wondrously called "the ark of the covenant of the Lord of all the earth."

The Ark was a simple "chest of acacia wood," speaking of the simple beauty of Jesus' humanity. The Ark was 3¾ feet long by 2¼ feet wide by 2¼ feet high (see Exod. 25:10). It is interesting to note that the top of the Ark where the atonement cover lay (2¼ feet from the ground), was at the exact same level as the grate halfway down in the altar of bronze on which the atoning sacrifice lay as it was being consumed in fire (see Exod. 27:1;4-5), thus binding the atoning sacrifice itself to the atonement cover, the mercy seat!

The Ark was overlaid "with pure gold, *both inside and out…*" (Exod. 25:11), a feature peculiar to the Ark, which speaks of the impeccable deity of our Lord, thoroughly woven throughout His entire being. The phrase "inside and out" is mentioned 21 times in Scripture, 7 × 3, speaking of the perfection of Jesus' divine nature—seven being the number of perfection and three being the number of God Himself. The ark was also crowned—"make a gold molding [a 'crown,' KJV] around it" (Exod. 25:11)—declaring Jesus to be "King of kings…" (Rev. 19:16).

The Ark was also a mobile unit. Exodus 25:12 states: "Cast four gold rings for it.…Then make poles of acacia wood and overlay them with gold. Insert the poles into the rings on the sides of the chest *to carry it.*" In all our journey, into all the world, to the very end of the age, Jesus Christ, our sufficient Savior is with us. Hallelujah!

The Lord then directed: "The poles ['staves,' KJV] are *to remain in the rings of the ark; they are not to be removed*" (Exod. 25:15). Since this was peculiar to the Ark of the Covenant, we must ask: why were these staves permanent? The probable reason was to facilitate the covering and the transport of the Ark. The mercy seat could never be looked upon by any man; even Aaron the high priest on the Day of Atonement could not look on the mercy seat: "He is to put the incense on the fire before the Lord, and the smoke of the incense will conceal the atonement cover above the Testimony, *so that he will not die*" (Lev. 16:13). So, when preparing the Ark to be moved, the priests would walk backwards with the veil, "the shielding curtain," and drape it over the Ark. The staves, permanently in place, would make it possible to prepare the Ark for being transported without anyone gazing on the mercy seat. This amplifies all the more the amazing grace of our God in providing such an open access to the Most Holy Place for *us today* through the blood of Jesus (see Heb. 10:19-22)!

"Then put in the ark *the Testimony,* which I will give you" (Exod. 25:16). The Testimony was a three-fold witness to our Lord Jesus Christ. Hebrews 9:4 explains this three-fold witness: "The gold-covered ark of the covenant...contained *the gold jar of manna, Aaron's staff that had budded,* and *the stone tablets of the covenant."*

In Exodus 16:33 the word was given: "Take a jar and put an omer of manna in it. Then place it before the Lord to be *kept for the generations* to come." This jar of manna was a part of the Testimony that would be kept safe in the Ark. This pot of manna itself was a miracle—it would be *"kept* for the generations to come," supernaturally kept as fresh and as new as the day it fell from heaven! (This is a notable miracle in light of Exodus 16:20, which states that the manna that was *"kept...until morning...was* full of maggots and began to smell"!)

Manna is spoken of 15 times in Scripture (3 × 5, symbolic of God's gracious gift). In Psalm 105:40 manna is called "the bread of heaven." And in John 6:48-51 Jesus declares:

> I am the bread of life. Your forefathers ate the manna in the desert, yet they died. But...**I am the living bread that came down from heaven.** If anyone eats of this bread, he will live forever....

Jesus is the true Manna. He is God's gracious gift of nourishment. He is the Bread of Heaven. Our unseen fellowship with Him is *"the hidden manna"* spoken of in Revelation 2:17. The manna in the golden pot bears testimony to Jesus, the Living Bread, ever fresh, ever new, from generation to generation, our nourishment and the mainstay of our lives!

Also in the Ark was "Aaron's staff that budded." The buds and blossoms and almonds on Aaron's staff bore witness to God's authentication of him and was to be part of the testimony in the Ark according to Numbers 17:8-11. The almond tree is symbolic of resurrection, and Romans 1:4 states that Jesus Christ our Lord, our greater Aaron, was "declared [attested] with power to be the Son of God *by His resurrection from the dead.*" This is a living testimony, authenticating our Lord Jesus Christ!

The third part of the testimony is "the stone tablets of the covenant." These were actually the second set of tablets of the law (see Exod. 34:1-4;28). The original tablets lay broken at the foot of Mount Sinai, a reflection of what Israel had done in breaking God's laws by their grievous idolatry (see Exod. 32:15-16;19). The second set would now remain *unbroken* in the Ark of the Covenant, a picture of God's holy law kept intact and unbroken in the person of our Lord Jesus Christ. He is the fulfillment of the prophetic words of Psalm 40:6-8:

> *Sacrifice and offering You did not desire...Then I said, "Here I am, I have come—it is written about Me in the scroll. I desire to do Your will, O My God;* **Your law is [intact] within My heart.**"

The threefold testimony in the Ark of the Covenant is the testimony of Jesus Christ. He is set forth as the Bread of Heaven, our unfailing sustenance. He is also declared with power to be the Son of God by His resurrection from the dead, and because He lives, we too shall live! And He is the One who fulfills the whole, unbroken law of God in us and through us!

The golden pot of manna and Aaron's rod that budded were witnesses to the Christ who accompanied Israel in all their wilderness journey (see 1 Cor. 10:3-4), but the holy law of God, the will of God, eternal in nature, rises above all time and endures forever. Probably for this reason, according to First Kings 8:9, only the tablets of stone were found in the Ark as it was placed in the permanent temple of Solomon.

"The Mercy Seat" (KJV) "The Atonement Cover" (NIV) (Exodus 25:17-22)

Above the Testimony was the mercy seat—ratifying, sealing, keeping the Testimony that was within the Ark. This golden plate covered the top of the Ark exactly (3¾ feet long by 2¼ feet wide), testifying to the sufficiency of the atonement to ensure us of all that was in the Testimony. All our need is completely and fully provided by our Lord Jesus Christ and guaranteed and satisfied by His atonement!

It was on this mercy seat once a year on the Day of Atonement that atonement was made for the sins of all Israel, according to Leviticus 16:11-19. Here is a picture of our Lord Jesus Christ entering "heaven itself, now to appear for us in God's presence…. He has appeared once for all at the end of the ages to do away with sin by the sacrifice of Himself" (Heb. 9:24-28).

The Hebrew word for "mercy seat" (KJV), or "atonement cover" (NIV), is *kapporeth,* used 27 times in Scripture (3 × 3 × 3). It means "covering." The Greek translation of the Old Testament, called the Septuagint, uses the word *hilasterion,* or propitiatory. As noted at the outset of this chapter, Romans 3:25 actually declares Jesus Himself to be our propitiatory, our mercy seat: "Christ Jesus whom God set forth [as] *a mercy seat* through faith in the blood…." What a wonderful thought! The expression "to make atonement" is used 77 times in the Old Testament. More than likely Jesus had this in His mind when He answered Peter's question:

> …"Lord, how many times shall I forgive my brother when he sins against me? Up to seven times?" Jesus answered, "I tell you, not seven times, but **seventy-seven** times" (Matthew 18:21-22).

Attached to either end of the mercy seat were the two cherubim.

> *Make two cherubim out of hammered gold at the ends of the cover…The cherubim are to have their wings spread upward, overshadowing the cover with them. The cherubim are to*

face each other, looking toward the cover. Place the cover on
top of the ark and put in the ark the Testimony, which I will
give you (Exodus 25:18-21).

Many students of Scripture believe the cherubim bore the four faces mentioned in Ezekiel 1:10—"the face of a man...the face of a lion...the face of an ox...the face of an eagle." These reflect the different facets of our Lord Jesus Christ, in His Humanity (the man), in His Kingship (the lion), in His Servanthood (the ox), and in His Deity (the eagle). These are the respective themes of the four gospels—Luke, Matthew, Mark, and John. The wings of the cherubim "spread upward, overshadowing the cover with them;" they covered, shielded, protected the mercy seat, similar to the way in which they protected the tree of life in the Garden of Eden (see Gen. 3:24). The cherubim faced each other in agreement, as they looked down toward the mercy seat. Peter probably had this in mind when he commented concerning the gospel that "even angels long *to look into these things*" (1 Pet. 1:12).

God is spoken of in Psalm 80:1 and 99:1 and Isaiah 37:16 as being *"enthroned* between the cherubim." The mercy seat was *the throne of God.* It is called "the throne of grace" in Hebrews 4:16, and we are encouraged to boldly draw near to that throne to receive mercy and find grace for ourselves!

God's Ultimate Intent

There, above the cover ["the mercy seat," KJV] *between the two cherubim that are over the ark of the Testimony,* **I will meet with you** *and give you all My commands for the Israelites* (Exodus 25:22).

God's ultimate intent was a return to Eden, a return to unbroken fellowship with man. "There...I will meet with you...." Here the "you" is clearly Moses. In Exodus 33:11 we are told, "The Lord would speak to Moses *face to face,* as a man speaks with his friend." What an awesome happening in Moses' life—"*I will meet with you.*"

But now those awesome close encounters are available to us all— "Let *us* then approach the throne of grace with *confidence,* so that *we* may receive mercy and find grace to help in *our* time of need" (Heb. 4:16). "*We* have *confidence* to enter the Most Holy Place by the blood of Jesus…*let us draw near to God* with a sincere heart in full assurance of faith…" (Heb. 10:19-22). This is God's ultimate intent for us, wonderfully realized through our Lord Jesus Christ!

PRAYER OF CONSECRATION

Lord Jesus Christ, I bless You for being my sacrificial Lamb, my propitiation, my Redeemer! Father, I thank You that You have opened a way for me into Your holy Presence through Jesus. Holy Spirit, I thank You that You now escort me past the outer court into the Holiest Place of all. By Your grace—Father, Son, and Holy Spirit—I will take my place before Your throne. I come into the Holy of Holies; I stand in Your unveiled Presence. Thank You! In Jesus' matchless Name. Amen.

ENDNOTE

1. A.B. Simpson, *Christ in the Tabernacle* (Camp Hill, PA: Christian Publications, 1987), p. 90.

Chapter 10

THE GLORIOUS FINALE

(Exodus 40:33-35)

A WILLING OFFERING

IN Exodus 25:2-8 the Lord instructed Moses:

*Tell the Israelites to **bring Me an offering.** You are to receive **the offering for Me** from each man **whose heart prompts him to give** ["from everyone who gives it willingly with his heart," NKJV]. These are the offerings you are to receive from them: gold, silver and bronze; blue, purple and scarlet yarn and fine linen; goat hair; ram skins dyed red and hides of sea cows; acacia wood; olive oil for the light; spices for the anointing oil and for the fragrant incense; and onyx stones and other gems to be mounted on the ephod and breastpiece. Then have them make **a sanctuary for Me,** and I will dwell among them.*

Exodus chapter 35 then described this grand offering for God's house:

*And everyone who was **willing** and **whose heart moved him** ["**whose heart was stirred,**" NKJV] came and brought* *an offering to the Lord for the work on the Tent of Meeting, for all its service, and for the sacred garments. All who were **willing** ["as many as had a willing heart," NKJV], men and women alike, came and brought gold jewelry of all kinds: brooches, earrings, rings and ornaments. They all presented their gold as a wave offering to the Lord* (Exodus 35:21-22).

These offerings were called *"freewill offerings"* (Exod. 35:29). They were *heart* offerings, *lovers'* offerings, for the house they would build for God to live in would be built in love! They gave "not reluctantly or under compulsion, for God loves a cheerful [literally, a *hilarious*] giver" (2 Cor. 9:7). And their giving was indeed hilarious! They were just so excited at the thought of God living in their midst! And so the people brought so much for the house, "more than enough," so that:

*Moses gave an order and they sent this word throughout the camp: "No man or woman is to make anything else as an offering for the sanctuary." And so the people were **restrained from bringing more,** because what they already had was **more than enough** to do all the work* (Exodus 36:5-7).

Not only did the people bring these valuable materials, they also donated their own time and talents—"Every skilled woman spun with her hands and brought what she had spun...and all the women who were willing and had the skill spun the goat hair" (Exod. 35:25-26). Besides these skilled women, God chose Bezalel of the tribe of Judah and "filled him with the Spirit of God, with skill, ability and knowledge in all kinds of crafts" (Exod. 35:31). Both Bezalel from Judah and Oholiab from Dan, who were master craftsmen, were given "the ability to teach others" (Exod. 34:34) in their respective skill sets—working with gold, silver and bronze and with stones and wood.

This section of Exodus reads like an Old Testament illustration of First Corinthians chapter 12:

*There are **different kinds of gifts,** but the same Spirit. There are **different kinds of service,** but the same Lord. There are*

different kinds of working, *but the same God works all of them in all men* (1 Corinthians 12:4-6).

As was true in the Old Testament house for the Lord, so it is now true in the New Testament house for the Lord. The Church of our Lord Jesus Christ is being built by a people passionate for the Presence of God—built by loving and generous, skillful and anointed hands as the members of Christ's Body are faithful to use the gifts and the graces and the resources that the Lord has given to each one.

Exodus 38:24-25 gives us an insight into the vastness of the monetary offerings given by the people for the Lord's house. "The total amount of the gold from the wave offering used for all the work on the sanctuary was 29 talents and 730 shekels" (that is, "a little over one ton," NIV margin). "The silver obtained from those of the community…was 100 talents and 1,775 shekels" (that is, "a little over 3¾ tons," NIV margin), nearly $30 million in gold and silver alone!

THE WEALTH OF SLAVES

The Lord had commanded: *"From what you have,* take an offering for the Lord" (Exod. 35:5). And we must ask, wherever did a band of slaves get so much wealth? Israel had lived in Egypt for four centuries, and for so much of that time they were slaves. "They put slave masters over them to oppress them with forced labor, and they built Pithom and Rameses as store cities for Pharaoh" (Exod. 1:11). How ever did *slaves* accumulate tens of millions of dollars in wealth?

In a prophetic word given to Abraham some 400 years earlier, the Lord had declared:

> *Know for certain that your descendants will be strangers in a country not their own, and they will be enslaved and mistreated four hundred years. But I will punish the nation they serve as slaves, and* ***afterward they will come out with great possessions*** (Genesis 15:13-14).

Four hundred years later, when the Lord commissioned Moses, He reiterated that promise:

> *I will stretch out My hand and strike the Egyptians with all the wonders that I will perform among them. After that, [Pharaoh] will let you go. And **I will make the Egyptians favorably disposed toward this people, so that when you leave you will not go empty-handed.** Every woman is to ask her neighbor and any woman living in her house for articles of silver and gold and for clothing, which you will put on your sons and daughters. And so you will plunder the Egyptians* (Exodus 3:20-22).

According to Exodus 11:2-3 and 12:35-36 that was exactly what happened—"they *plundered* the Egyptians"! The KJV states "they *spoiled* the Egyptians"! As the contemporary song declares, they went down to the enemy's camp and took back what he stole from them—400 years of back wages for all their forced labor for having built Pithom and Rameses as store cities for Pharaoh! Four hundred years worth of reparations for the resources and vitality that the enemy forcibly had taken from them!

It is interesting to view all of this in the light of what would then become an established law in Israel:

> *If a fellow Hebrew, a man or a woman, sells himself to you and serves you six years, in the seventh year you must let him go free. And **when you release him, do not send him away empty-handed.** Supply him liberally from your flock, your threshing floor and your winepress. Give to him as the Lord your God has blessed you. **Remember that you were slaves in Egypt and the Lord your God redeemed you. That is why I give you this command today*** (Deuteronomy 15:12-15).

Many in our own American society have been similarly taken advantage of and even enslaved—all the way from First Nation's people to the slaves brought from Africa to work the plantations. The mandates of Deuteronomy 15:12-15 surely apply to them! And many others—women, minorities, youth, and children—have also been exploited and taken advantage of in the calculating and cold world of business. Though we cannot always make legal claims of redress for the way in which we have been defrauded, we can engage in spiritual warfare against those principalities and powers who are in back of such evil, and we can go down to the enemy's camp and take back what he stole from us! That unexpected raise, that surprise bonus, that new job offer, that unanticipated inheritance—all of it may be exactly *how* the Lord gives back to us what the enemy has stolen. Let us believe God for such miraculous returns!

"One Thing—Is What I Seek!"

Moses was a man with a quest for the glory of God. He delighted in the Presence of God! He longed for the manifest reality of His God. He was an earlier version of David, who wrote:

> One thing I ask of the Lord, this is what I seek: that I may dwell in the house of the Lord...to gaze upon the beauty of the Lord and to seek Him...At His tabernacle will I sacrifice with shouts of joy; I will sing and make music to the Lord (Psalm 27:4,6).

Exodus 40:17 states that "the tabernacle was set up on the first day of the first month in the second year." The skilled workers, building the golden house for the Lord, had labored much of that first year after their exodus from Egypt. And it was a labor of love! "The Israelites did *everything just as the Lord commanded* Moses" (Exod. 39:32). "And so Moses finished the work" (Exod. 40:33). The divine compound was completed.

It is important to note that, at its completion, there were six pieces of furniture in the three courts of the Tabernacle—the bronze altar of burnt offering plus the bronze laver in the outer court; the golden lampstand, the golden table of the bread of the Presence, and the golden altar of incense in the Holy Place; and the Ark of the Testimony in the Holy of Holies. Four of these pieces were positioned in a straight line from east to west—eastward was the bronze altar of burnt offering, then in line was the bronze laver, next the golden altar of incense, and westward was the Ark of the Testimony. The remaining two of these six pieces of furniture were placed in a straight line from north to south: the golden table of the bread of the Presence to the north and the golden lampstand to the south. All six pieces formed the sign of a cross as one looked down upon these six pieces of furniture! So far, so good.

However, the disconcerting matter was that there were only *six* pieces of furniture in this house and *six is the number of incompleteness.* After all had been said and done, the task was *yet unfinished.* Even though "Moses finished [his] work," God Himself needed to add *the seventh piece* to complete the house. And so it was that:

> **Then** *the cloud covered the Tent of Meeting, and **the glory of the Lord** filled the tabernacle. Moses could not enter the Tent of Meeting because the cloud had settled upon it, and the glory of the Lord filled the tabernacle* (Exodus 40:34-35).

The glorious Presence of Jehovah completed the house! For apart from that glory the house was yet unfinished; it was yet incomplete.

How valuable a lesson for the Church of our Lord Jesus Christ. Apart from God's manifest and glorious Presence in our midst the house will be incomplete; its walls will ring hollow; its rooms will be empty. The Presence of the Lord *Himself* is what makes the house, the House of *God!*

Communion with God, intimacy with the Most High, living life in the light of God's glorious Presence—this has always been the passionate quest of all spiritual men and women. God *walked* in the garden with Adam and Eve (see Gen. 3:8). That's how the human story began. The Hebrew word translated "walked" is *halak,* meaning "to *go on habitually,* to *go up and down.*"[1]

Enoch, "the seventh from Adam" (Jude 14) consequently *walked on habitually* with God—"up and down," "ascending and descending" (John 1:51) in the Presence of his God. According to the genealogy of Genesis chapter 5, Adam, Enoch's great forebear, was *still alive* when Enoch was growing up. It is easy to believe that as the young boy Enoch would sit at the feet of the aging patriarch, Adam, and hear him recount the wonders of *walking with God,* a hunger was created in him for that same intimacy with God. And so it is recorded twice that "Enoch *walked with God*" (Gen. 5:22 and 24). Enoch's life in God's Presence impacted his great grandson, Noah, who also *"walked with God"* (Gen. 6:9). The pursuit of the Presence of God became a generational legacy.

I can only pray that my four grandsons, Chase Patrick and Kai Francis and Dylan Charles and Hunter Scott, and my lovely granddaughter, Brooke Morgan, will also *walk habitually with God, "ascending and descending"* in the Presence of God. That is the generational legacy I wish to leave behind!

Abraham was likewise a man who *walked habitually with God* as did Noah and Enoch his forbearers (see Gen. 17:1; 24:40), and Isaac, his son after him, *walked before God* (see Gen. 48:15). These were men of God's Presence! The *God of glory* had appeared to Abraham according to Stephen's account of Abraham's life in Acts 7:2. And that experience of the Presence of God created in Abraham a hunger for God Himself.

Abraham, in renaming the city of Luz *Bethel,* the House of God, consequently began the quest for building a dwelling place for God. Abraham was not satisfied for a mere *visitation from God;* he hungered for a *habitation for God*—a place where God could dwell, a place where He could be visited, that secret place where He could be found! Jacob, Abraham's grandson, carried on that glorious pursuit—"this stone that I have set up as a pillar will be *God's house...*" (Gen. 28:22). And now Moses had carried the vision to a new level as "the cloud of the Lord was over the tabernacle by day, and fire was in the cloud by night, in the sight of all the house of Israel during all their travels" (Exod. 40:38).

This passion would be carried to yet another level by David and the magnificent house that he commissioned Solomon his son to build—*a house for God's excellent glory!* And all of this would find its eventual fulfillment in our Lord Jesus Christ, the Man of glory. "We have seen His glory, the glory of the One and Only, who came from the Father, full of grace and truth" (John 1:14).

And now He has raised up a people in the earth, His holy dwelling place, a people who literally "[shine] with the glory of God" (Rev. 21:11)! This has been God's passion all along; this has been what He intended from the beginning. This is the eternal purpose of our God in Christ Jesus our Lord—that God should dwell among men! "Now the dwelling [the tabernacle] of God is with men, and He will live with them. They will be His people, and God Himself will be with them and be their God" (Rev. 21:3)!

PRAYER OF CONSECRATION

Lord of Heaven, I am willing in the day of Your power! The resources, the giftings, the ministry-anointing You have given me by Your grace, I offer up to You that Your House, Your Church, might be built in this generation!

I offer myself to You to be a person of Your Presence, to be as Adam and Enoch and Abraham and Jacob and Moses and David, as I hunger for You, for Your Glory, for intimacy with You! Take my life and let it be consecrated, Lord, to You. I pray in Jesus' Name. Amen.

ENDNOTE

1. Robert Young, LL.D., *Analytical Concordance to the Holy Bible* (London: Latterworth Press, 1953), p. 1031—"to go on habitually or up and down; halak."

Chapter 11

THE FESTIVALS OF
THE LORD

AT the very beginning of the instruction about building a house for the Lord, the Lord gives this command:

> *Three times a year you are to **celebrate** a festival to Me. **Celebrate** the Feast of Unleavened Bread...**Celebrate** the Feast of Harvest with the firstfruits of the crops you sow in your field. **Celebrate** the Feast of Ingathering at the end of the year, when you gather in your crops from the field. Three times a year all the men are to appear before the Sovereign Lord* (Exodus 23:14-17).

And again, right in the middle of the construction of the Tabernacle, the Lord speaks a second time:

> ***Celebrate** the Feast of Unleavened Bread...**Celebrate** the Feast of Weeks with the firstfruits of the wheat harvest, and the Feast of Ingathering at the turn of the year. Three times a year all your men are to appear before the Sovereign Lord, the God of Israel* (Exodus 34:18-23).

God's house was to be *a house of celebration!* At least three times in a year, *a holy party* would be thrown by God for His people! The first celebration in Israel began "in the month of Abib, for in that month you came out of Egypt" (Exod. 23:15; 34:18). When the prodigal came out of his own personal bondage and returned to his father's house in Luke 15:20-24, the comment was made "So they began *to celebrate*" (Luke 15:24). *The Book* translates that phrase, "So *the party* began." The festivals of the Lord are a call to holy celebration, an invitation to the parties that Heaven has called!

Two very interesting Hebrew words appear in the introductory verses of Leviticus 23, the chapter outlining Jehovah's festivals. In Leviticus 23:2 and then throughout the chapter, the Lord said, "Speak to the Israelites, and say to them: 'These are My appointed feasts, the appointed feasts of the Lord, which you are to proclaim as *sacred assemblies* ["*holy convocations*," KJV].'" The Hebrew word translated "assemblies" or "convocations" is *miqra* (mik-raw), and one of its meanings is "*rehearsals*," according to *Strong's Exhaustive Concordance.*[1] The festivals of Jehovah were holy rehearsals!

I recently took note of a secular sign that read: "Live life; this is not a rehearsal!" For a materialistic unbeliever that might be true, but for the believer the exact opposite is true. We are to live life realizing that *this is a rehearsal.* We are rehearsing for the future; life is a dress rehearsal for a Kingdom about to be unveiled that shall never pass away!

The second Hebrew word that caught my eye is found in Leviticus 23:6 and then throughout the chapter: "On the fifteenth day of [the first] month the Lord's *Feast* of Unleavened Bread begins...." According to Strong's, the word translated "*feast*" is *chag*, from *chagag* (khaw-gag), meaning "to move in a circle; to celebrate, to dance, to reel to and fro."[2] What excellent definition these two Hebrew words give to these festivals of Jehovah! They are *dress rehearsals* of things to come; and they are *celebrations* with dancing and reeling to and fro in ecstatic joy! Real parties! On this backdrop let us consider these *three* main celebrations of Jehovah, comprised of *seven* wonderful festivals. And in our study of these festivals let us keep in mind Paul's principle of interpretation in Colossians 2:17; these festivals are "shadows of the real thing—of *Christ Himself*" (TLB).

According to Leviticus chapter 23 there are three main celebrations. Two are spring celebrations: Passover and Pentecost; the other, Tabernacles, is a fall celebration. We will begin with a general overview of these celebrations with more details on each to follow in the next chapters.

PASSOVER

In the middle of the first month of Israel's calendar year (our March or April) the Festival of Passover was to be celebrated. It marked Israel's New Year. Passover is a picture of "Christ, our Passover Lamb...sacrificed" for us (1 Cor. 5:7-8). Passover was actually a three-in-one festival. For seven days unleavened bread was eaten, which speaks of the holiness that the death and resurrection of Jesus produces in us. The Passover lamb was slain and eaten and the lamb's blood applied to each house, speaking of the work of Calvary. Finally, on the first Sunday after Passover, firstfruits from the spring barley harvest were waved before God, which speak of the resurrection of the Lamb of God on Resurrection Sunday (see 1 Cor. 15:2-23).

This glorious festival in its three parts—Unleavened bread, Passover, and Firstfruits—has been fulfilled by Jesus in His first coming, by His death, and by His resurrection. Now our joy is to celebrate His finished work for us!

PENTECOST

In the third month (our May or June), the Festival of Pentecost, or the Feast of Weeks, was celebrated. Pentecost was a celebration of the giving of the Law and is fulfilled by the holy Law of God being written on the tables of our hearts through God filling us with His Holy Spirit. Acts chapter 2, the Day of Pentecost, is the historical fulfillment of this festival. And our joy is to celebrate this outpouring of the Holy Spirit as *we ourselves* are filled with the Holy Spirit!

The Fall Festivals

After a long, dry summer interval, the fall festivals of the Lord took place in the seventh month. "Seven" is the month of *completion,* corresponding to our September–October. In these fall festivals we find the *completion* of Jesus' great work, bringing us to His Second Coming. The two spring festivals of Passover and Pentecost show us what Jesus *did* when He came the first time; the fall festivals now show us what Jesus *is doing* as He prepares us for His Second Coming. As with Passover, the fall festivals are also a "three-in-one" happening.

On the first day of the seventh month is the day of blowing trumpets (see Lev. 23:23-25). This is called in Hebrew *Yom Teruah.* And so God is presently giving us, His people, the blasts of His holy trumpet to awaken us and to prepare us for His last-days visitation! (Israel has taken this day as a second New Year—*Rosh Hashanah.*)

On the tenth day of the seventh month, after ten days of soul-searching repentance and holy "awe," came the Day of Atonement, *Yom Kippur.* Yom Kippur was the outworking of the Passover (see Lev. 16:29-30). We can, therefore, expect to see a great worldwide application of the blood of Jesus in these last days, a worldwide revival. The Day of Atonement involves two goats—one slain, with its blood sprinkled on the Mercy Seat in the Holy of Holies, and the other, the Scapegoat, let loose in the wilderness to "carry our sins far, far away." These two goats speak to us of Jesus in His death and in His resurrection carrying away our sins.

The climax of these fall feasts, Tabernacles, or *Succoth* in Hebrew, began on the 15th day of the seventh month and lasted for seven days. During these final seven days, the people of God lived in "booths" or "tabernacles" or "tents" as a continual reminder that they were a pilgrim people. These days were also days of great rejoicing by a pilgrim people for *the greatest harvest of the year!* This points to our rejoicing in these last days over the greatest ingathering of souls the people of God have ever seen! (see James 5:7-8).

The finale of this festival is recorded for us in John 7:37-39 on "the Last Day, the greatest day of the feast." On this day, water was drawn from the pool of Siloam and poured out in the Temple, picturing the end-time *outpouring of the Holy Spirit* that makes the end-time harvest possible (see Acts 2:17-21). And the grand finale of this festival is *Simchat Torah*, the joyful celebration of the union of the people of God to the Torah. This celebration has been called "the happiest day of the year" for it prefigures the Marriage Supper of the Lamb, when Jesus, the living Word, shall come and take His glorious Bride to be with Him forever!

All of these great prophetic pictures are given to us to inspire our faith in these last days as we witness God's great outpouring and worldwide harvest just before the coming of the great and notable Day of the Lord!

Two Final Biblical Festivals

Leviticus chapter 23 describes these three main celebrations comprised of seven festivals. These three celebrations, the seven festivals, take place at God's house, as given by the Lord to Moses. As the Scriptures unfold, however, we can trace two more biblical festivals in the latter years of Israel's Old Testament history—the Festival of Purim and the Festival of Hanukkah. We want to consider them briefly before we return in detail to the original festivals of the Tabernacle given to Moses.

The Festival of Purim

The story of Purim is told in the Book of Esther, the final historical book in the canon of Holy Scripture. The word *purim* is a Persian word meaning "lots." The stories of Purim and of Esther take place in Persia (modern-day Iran) around the year 475 B.C.

The first of four main players in the story of Purim was the Persian Emperor Xerxes I ["Ahasuerus," as in the KJV, is Hebrew for a title meaning "majesty"; Xerxes was the emperor's Persian given name]. The second main player was Esther, whose Hebrew given name was *Hadassah,* which means "myrtle." Hadassah, in an attempt to conceal her Jewish identity, took the name *Esther* from the Babylonian goddess Ishtar, the Queen of Heaven (see Jer. 7:18). This Esther was chosen to replace the deposed Persian empress Vashti, and so became the favored wife of Xerxes the Persian emperor.

The third main player was Haman, the Agagite, a man whose family apparently had survived the slaughter of the Amalekites in Israel in First Samuel 15:7-9. This Haman, prime minister of the Persian Court, with a deep hatred for the Jews who had brought such devastation on his people, plotted the extermination of the whole Jewish race (see Esther 3:13). The date for this holocaust was chosen by lot *(pur)* to be "the thirteenth day of the twelfth month, the month Adar" (Esther 9:1).

The fourth main player in this drama of Purim was Mordecai, a cousin of Esther (see Esther 2:7), who became the inspiration to Esther to make known her Jewish identity to the emperor and to appear before him to plead for the life of her people. This she did and the Jews were spared. Haman and his sons were executed, and Mordecai, Esther's cousin, was honored, replacing Haman as prime minister of the Persian Court.

On the very day that the Jews were slated for extermination, the thirteenth day of the month of Adar, the tables were turned and the Jews overcame and defeated their enemies. And that day and the day following became known as the Festival of Purim among the Jews, the festival of God's deliverance of His people through the boldness of one young Jewish girl, Hadassah.

Esther (Hadassah) becomes a model for us as the people of God, to rise up in faith out of any compromise and any fear in these last days, to become as bold as a lion in confronting the insidious forces of darkness that are covering the earth.

One of the puzzling things about the Book of Esther is that (seemingly) nowhere in its pages does the Name of God appear. It is almost as if *He is not there,* yet He *is* there, standing in the shadows, working out His sovereign plan! And amazingly scholars have found the Sacred Tetragrammaton (YHWH), from which we get God's holy Name Yahweh or Jehovah, to be *hidden five times* in acrostic form (in Esther 1:17,20; 5:4,13; and 7:7). In three of the ancient manuscripts these letters in these acrostics are written larger than the rest of the text so as to stand out boldly on the scroll. Though seemingly hidden from view, God is yet very much present and very active—a promise for us in these last days!

HANUKKAH

The final feast of the latter Old Testament is *Hanukkah,* which means "dedication." It is referred to in John 10:22-23 as "the Feast of Dedication." It is also known as the "Festival of Lights," because of the small amount of sacred oil which miraculously lasted for a full eight days, causing the menorah to continue to burn.

The story of Hanukkah is told prophetically in the Book of Daniel. Because of the sins of God's people, the Babylonians, under Nebuchadnezzar, had subjugated the Holy Land in 605 B.C. (see Dan. 1:1). But the Babylonian empire was then overthrown by the Medes and the Persians in 539 B.C., and the Persians, in turn, were defeated at Issus by Alexander the Great of Greece in 333 B.C. (see Dan. 5:30-31; 8:5-7;20-21). After a 12-year career of military brilliance, Alexander the Great died, leaving his empire to be divided among his four generals (see Dan. 8:8,22). Antipater with his son Cassander reigned over Macedonia and Greece, Lysimachus over Thrace and Asia Minor, Ptolemy I over Palestine and Egypt, and Seleucus I over Syria.[3]

The "horn" described in Daniel 8:9, eventually coming from the Seleucid dynasty of Syria, was Antiochus IV Theos Epiphanes (meaning "god manifest"). In late 168 B.C. Antiochus Epiphanes began a campaign against the Holy Land ("the Beautiful Land") that eventuated in the conquest of the Temple Mount and the desecration of the Holy Sanctuary (see Dan. 8:11-12). Antiochus placed an idol of Zeus

Olympius in the Holy of Holies, blasphemously defiling the most Holy Place. However, after "2,300 evenings and mornings" (Dan. 8:14), 1,150 days, or three years and two months, the Temple mount was recaptured by the Maccabees, a band of freedom-fighters who drove the Syrian invaders from their land. The Temple site was then "consecrated" by the Maccabees on December 25, 165 B.C. (see Dan. 8:14).

This consecration or dedication was known as *Hanukkah*. And it was believed that at that time God performed the miracle of multiplying the holy oil for eight days until new oil could be prepared. In honor of the eight miracle days, the Hanukkah menorah has eight lamps instead of the original seven prescribed by Moses in the Tabernacle. Over the eight days of Hanukkah one lamp is lit each night by a *ninth* lamp called the *Shamash,* which means "the Servant." The Shamash is taken and lowered to light each of the lamps throughout the eight days, a picture of the Servant of Jehovah, the Messiah, who comes in His lowliness to bring light to us that we might shine for the glory of God! Many believe that the miraculous conception of our Lord Jesus, "the true light that gave light to every man" (John 1:9), took place on this 25th day of December, corresponding to our Christmas, and that His actual birth nine months later took place during the Festival of Lights during the Feast of Tabernacles in the fall of the year.

AN END-TIME PICTURE

Even though Antiochus IV Theos Epiphanes ("god manifest") had been dead for nearly 200 years, Jesus, in Matthew 24:15-16, treated the events of this beast's desecration of the Holy Place as *yet future,* a concept intimated by the prophecies of Daniel 9:27 and Daniel 11:31-32;35. Paul, in Second Thessalonians 2:3-4, likewise treated the abominations of Antiochus Epiphanes as having a *future* fulfillment in the last days. The predictions of Matthew 24 along with Second Thessalonians 2 give us grounds to believe that Antiochus IV Theos Epiphanes was but a type and a shadow of the future Antichrist, the man of sin, the "beast" of the last days. That being the case, we can see in the Maccabees a type and a shadow of an end-time band of freedom-fighters who "do know their God [and] shall be strong, and do exploits" (Dan. 11:32 KJV)! Revelation 12:11 describes these overcomers in these words: "They overcame [satan] by the blood of the Lamb and by the word of their testimony; they did not love their lives so much as to shrink from death."

In the final battle of the ages, when the antichrist and his followers:

> *...will make war against the Lamb...the Lamb will overcome them because He is Lord of lords and King of kings—and with Him will be His **called, chosen and faithful followers*** (Revelation 17:14)!

These are God's end-time guerrilla warriors who "put on the full armor of God, so that when the day of evil comes, [they] may be able to stand [their] ground, and after [they] have done everything, to stand... firm..." (Eph. 6:13-14).

What deep personal challenges come to us from these two final festivals—Purim and Hanukkah: challenges to a radical consecration to the Lord and to His purposes in these last days!

PRAYER OF CONSECRATION

Great Warrior of Heaven, we do rise up in Your Name as Esther Your servant did and as the Maccabees, Your freedom fighters, did to stand against the spirit of this crooked and depraved age, as You bring in everlasting righteousness! We thank You that we shall shortly see satan crushed beneath our feet as the kingdoms of this world become the Kingdom of our Lord and of His Christ! And You shall reign forever and ever! Hallelujah! In Jesus' Name. Amen.

Now let us return to the three celebrations of Leviticus chapter 23 and consider them in detail.

ENDNOTES

1. James Strong, *Strong's Exhaustive Concordance of the Bible* (Nashville/New York: Abingdon Press, 1973), *miqra* #4744 on page 71 of Hebrew Dictionary.

2. *Strong's Concordance*, #2282 and #2287, *chag/chagog* on page 37 of Hebrew Dictionary.

3. World history confirms these facts. Some of this information can be found on page 1310 of the NIV Study Bible in the footnote on Daniel 7:4-7.

Chapter 12

THE EARLY SPRING FESTIVALS OF PASSOVER, UNLEAVENED BREAD, AND FIRSTFRUITS

CLUSTERED around the first spring celebration are three festivals: the sacrifice of *the Passover Lamb,* a picture of the Lamb of God sacrificed for us; the weeklong *Festival of Unleavened Bread,* a picture of the sanctifying work of the cross purging the leaven of sin from our lives that we might be an unleavened loaf; and finally, the *Festival of Firstfruits* in which the first ripe sheaf from the barley harvest was waved before the Lord on that first Sunday after Passover, a picture of the rising again of our Lord Jesus Christ on Resurrection Sunday after His Crucifixion. This first spring celebration is about the first coming of our Lord Jesus Christ, His sacrificial death, and His triumphant resurrection! Let us consider it in detail.

THE PASSOVER

Passover comes from the Hebrew word *pesach,* meaning to "pass over." "When I see the blood, I will *pass over* you. No destructive plague will touch you when I strike Egypt" (Exod. 12:13). Passover was the celebration of the marvelous deliverance of the people of God from their bondage to Egypt.

"The Lord's Passover begins at twilight on the fourteenth day of *the first month*" (Lev. 23:5). Passover marked *the beginning* of the history of God's people: "This month shall be unto you *the beginning of months:* it shall be *the first month* of the year to you" (Exod. 12:2 KJV). The Passover marked Israel's spiritual New Year. And so Calvary, our great deliverance from bondage through Christ Jesus the Lamb of God, marks the *beginning* of our own personal salvation history in God!

Paul clearly interprets the Passover festival for us in his words to the Corinthians: "Christ, our Passover lamb, has been sacrificed. Therefore let us keep the Festival..." (1 Cor. 5:7-8). Passover is all about Jesus! As a festival it was "a shadow of the things that were to come; the reality, however, is found in *Christ*" (Col. 2:16-17).

"Each man is to take a lamb for his family, *one for each household*" (Exod. 12:3). These words remind us of the important happenings at Philippi as Paul ministered the gospel in that city. Concerning Lydia, the dealer in purple cloth: "The Lord opened her heart to respond to Paul's message...[and] she and *the members of her household* were baptized..." (Acts 16:14-15). To the Philippian jailor this most wonderful promise was given: "Believe in the Lord Jesus, and you will be saved—*you and your household*" (Acts 16:31). And that promise was abundantly fulfilled: "He and *all his family* were baptized...The jailer... was filled with joy because he had come to believe in God—he and *his whole family*" (Acts 16:33-34).

As we individually come to Christ, it then becomes our joy to declare "a lamb for a household," and to claim in believing prayer our mother and our father, our sister and our brother, our children and our grandchildren for Christ! God wills that *our entire households* be brought under the saving canopy of *the blood* of the Lamb of God!

"The animals *you choose* must be year-old males *without defect*" (Exod. 12:5). Peter speaks of Jesus as that "lamb *without blemish or defect...chosen* before the creation of the world" (1 Pet. 1:19-20)—chosen by God our Father, a sufficient lamb for His entire household!

"*Take care of them* until the fourteenth day of the month, when all the people of the community of Israel must slaughter them at twilight" (Exod. 12:6). "Take care of them…" brings to mind Nathan's story:

> …*the poor man [who] had nothing except one little ewe lamb… He raised it, and it grew up with him and his children. It shared his food, drank from his cup and even slept in his arms. It was like a daughter to him* (2 Samuel 12:3).

O, the deep emotional attachment this picture paints for us! The whole purpose of the household "taking care" of that spotless yearling Passover lamb for a number of days was to foster just that same kind of emotional attachment to the little lamb. Can't you just see the children playing with the little lamb, feeding it, holding it close? Can't you just see the deep pain as the family sees that spotless little lamb *slaughtered* at sunset on that fourteenth day? Our Father would have us enter in some small way into the deep pain that He Himself endured as He offered up Heaven's Darling to be slaughtered for the sins of the world!

The little lamb was slaughtered "at twilight." We are reminded of Amos' words concerning that day: "I will make the sun go down at noon and darken the earth in broad daylight" (Amos 8:9). That is the way it happened on Golgotha's hill for you and for me! "Look, the Lamb of God, who takes away the sin of the world!" (John 1:29).

> *Take a bunch of hyssop, dip it into the blood in the basin and put some of the blood* **on the top and on both sides of the doorframe…** *When the Lord goes through the land to strike down the Egyptians, He will see the blood on the top and sides of the doorframe and will pass over that doorway, and He will not permit the destroyer to enter your houses and strike you down* (Exodus 12:22-23).

The blood was to be placed on the top, or lintel (KJV), of the doorframe and on both sides of the doorframe, making the sign of the cross on each home that would experience deliverance. The blood was never

to be put on the threshold where people could trample on it; hence, the warning sounded in Hebrews 10:29:

> *How much more severely do you think a man deserves to be punished who has trampled the Son of God under foot, who has treated as an unholy thing the blood of the covenant that sanctified him, and who has insulted the Spirit of grace?*

When we honor the power of the blood, God assures us: "I will *pass over* you. No destructive plague will touch you..." (Exod. 12:13).

> *That same night they are to* **eat the meat** *roasted over the fire* [fire speaking of God's judgment against sin], *along with bitter herbs* [bitter speaking of the intense suffering and agony of that sacrifice], *and bread made without yeast* [unleavened speaking of the sanctifying work of the Spirit of grace coming from that sacrifice]. *Do not eat the meat raw* [the sacrifice was not valid without the fires of judgment] *or cooked in water* [the sacrifice was never to be diluted or watered down], *but* **roast it over the fire—head,**

legs and inner parts...Eat it in haste; it is the Lord's Passover (Exodus 12:8-9,11).

We note that the "inner parts" or entrails were part of this sacrifice. Students of the Passover have described how the entrails of the lamb were wrapped around its head as it was roasted in the fire, making it a "crowned sacrifice."

Chapter 7, verse 1 of *The Pesachim* states that a wooden pomegranate spit was thrust lengthwise through the lamb. Justin Martyr (in *Trypho*, 40) reports that another spit was put crosswise, to which the front feet were attached, actually binding the lamb to the two spits in the form of a cross. "So do the modern Samaritans in roasting the Passover lamb..." records the *Bible Encyclopedia and Dictionary* by A.R. Fausset. Awesome detailed pictures of Calvary's sacrifice!

The lamb was to be eaten by a people prepared for immediate departure from bondage. Thus the community of Israel was told to eat "with your cloak tucked into your belt, your sandals on your feet and your staff in your hand. Eat it *in haste*..." (Exod. 12:11). Jesus stuns us with His insistence:

*Unless you **eat the flesh of the Son of Man** and drink His blood, you have no life in you. Whoever **eats My flesh** and drinks My blood has eternal life...* [and] *remains in Me, and I in him* (John 6:53-54;56).

Jesus indeed is the Lord's Passover; He is our deliverance meal! And through His strength we are enabled to flee the bondage of this present evil age. "This day shall be unto you for *a memorial*" (Exod. 12:14 KJV). Jesus, during His final earthly Passover meal, instituted His Table for the Church *as a memorial*: "Do this *in remembrance of Me*" (Luke 22:19); *do this that you never forget Me!* "This day shall be unto you for *a memorial*"!

Finally, the Israelites were commanded: "Do not break any of the bones" (Exod. 12:46; Num. 9:12).

*When they came to Jesus and found that He was already dead, **they did not break His legs**...These things happened so that the Scripture would be fulfilled: "Not one of His bones will be broken"* (John 19:33,36).

It is utterly amazing to see how our Lord Jesus Christ in His sacrifice on the cross fulfilled *every* single aspect of the Passover in Himself! Indeed "Christ, our Passover, was sacrificed for us" (1 Cor. 5:7 NKJV).

THE FEAST OF UNLEAVENED BREAD

*For seven days you are to eat **bread made without yeast**... Celebrate the Feast of Unleavened Bread, because it was on this very day that I brought your divisions* ["armies," KJV] *out of Egypt...* (Exodus 12:15,17).

Paul unfolds for us the deep spiritual significance of this second festival that surrounded the Passover; in his words to the Corinthians: "Therefore let us keep the Festival, not with the old yeast, the yeast of malice and wickedness, but with bread without yeast, the bread of sincerity and truth" (1 Cor. 5:8). Jesus is our slain Passover Lamb and

He brings us, by His redeeming grace, into a life of sanctification—a life without "the yeast of malice and wickedness," an unleavened life of "sincerity and truth." *Truth* can be defined as a state of genuineness, honesty, and reality. *Sincerity* can be defined as being without deceit, pretense, or hypocrisy; *being the same in actual character as in outward appearance.* This is what it means to be an unleavened loaf!

The Passover has been diligently celebrated by Israel throughout the past millennia. Even early Christian believers celebrated the Passover as a prophetic picture of Jesus the Lamb of God until it was outlawed in the fourth century by the Roman Emperor Constantine. The Passover, as it is celebrated today in Jewish homes and among Christians around the world, evidences the strong influence that early Messianic believers had on this celebration.

This is most evident in that part of the Passover Seder that deals with *the unleavened bread, the matzah.* Three pieces of matzah are placed on the table wrapped in a matzah tosh. The middle matzah is particularly intriguing. At one juncture in the ceremony this middle matzah is broken, and one of the broken pieces is wrapped in a white cloth and hidden out of sight. At the end of the Seder the children search for this "buried" piece of matzah. The children are promised a gift from the father when they find it. The gift is called "the promise of the father," given to the one who finds the hidden piece of matzah.

How clearly can we see messianic truth in this part of the ceremony! The matzah tosh with three pieces of matzah pictures our Triune God—Father, Son, and Holy Spirit. The middle matzah which is broken, wrapped in a cloth, and "buried," pictures the Son, our Lord Jesus Christ. God's children are commissioned to seek Him, and are given the promise of a gift upon finding Him. "Wait for the gift My Father promised…for John baptized with water, but in a few days you will be baptized with the Holy Spirit" (Acts 1:4-5).

*The Passover and the Feast of Unleavened Bread are "for you **and your descendants**…And when **your children** ask you, 'What does this ceremony mean to you?' then tell them,*

'It is the Passover sacrifice to the Lord, who passed over the houses of the Israelites in Egypt...'" (Exodus 12:24;26-27).

THE WAVING OF THE FIRSTFRUITS

Israel was told:

Bring to the priest a sheaf of the first grain you harvest. He is to wave the sheaf before the Lord so it will be accepted on your behalf; the priest is to wave it on the day after the Sabbath (Leviticus 23:10-11).

The final festival of this first spring celebration was the waving of the first sheaf of the barley harvest as a declaration that the full harvest was coming. This firstfruits celebration on the first day of the week following the slaying of the Passover lamb was fulfilled on Resurrection Sunday when our Lord Jesus Christ was raised from the dead by the glory of the Father. In First Corinthians 15:23 Paul consequently calls our Lord Jesus: *"Christ, the firstfruits"* and then describes the full harvest that is coming: "when He comes, [with Him will be] those who belong to Him."

The waving of the barley sheaf before the God of Heaven on that first Sunday after Passover may shed light on the interaction between Jesus and Mary in John 20:16-17 on Resurrection morning. Later Jesus had no problem with Thomas touching Him (John 20:27), but in His earlier time with Mary He said to her, *"Touch Me not; for I am not yet ascended to My Father..."* (John 20:17 KJV). From these words we may believe that Jesus ascended to the Father *that very morning* to present Himself before Him as the Firstfruits of the harvest to come and then returned for the 40 days before His final and permanent ascension.

O, the wonder of this first spring celebration with its three interwoven festivals—Passover, Unleavened Bread, and Firstfruits—all speaking to us of the death and resurrection of our Lord Jesus Christ and of the sanctifying grace that comes to us through His redeeming work! Paul consequently begins First Corinthians chapter 15 with the grand declaration: "Christ [as our Passover Lamb] died for our sins according to the Scriptures…He was buried…He was raised [as the Firstfruits] on the third day according to the Scriptures…" (1 Cor. 15:3-4). This is the good news! Praise God for such a wonderful salvation!

PRAYER OF CONSECRATION

Lord Jesus Christ, I do receive Your death for my salvation. You are my Passover Lamb. I shelter myself and my whole household beneath Your protecting blood. I take into my heart and life Your sanctifying grace that I might be an unleavened loaf. And I rejoice in Your resurrection and in the amazing thought that I have been raised with You to walk in newness of life. Thank You, Lord Jesus Christ! Amen.

Chapter 13

THE LATER SPRING FESTIVAL
OF PENTECOST

THE second spring festival was called the "Feast of Weeks" because it came seven full weeks and one day (50 days) after Firstfruits Sunday. Another name for this festival was Pentecost, which means "the fiftieth day." In Exodus 23:16 it was called "the Feast of Harvest" in celebration of the late spring wheat harvest.

This festival originally commemorated the giving of the Law at Mount Sinai 50 days after the Passover, the day of Israel's exodus from Egypt. The fulfillment of this type and shadow was the Day of Pentecost recorded for us in Acts chapter 2, in which the Holy Spirit came anew from Heaven inscribing God's holy law not on tables of stone but on the hearts and minds of His people. "I will put My law in their minds and write it on their hearts..." (Jer. 31:33) was the Pentecostal promise. The Old Testament type of Pentecost celebrated an old covenant; the New Testament fulfillment, the Day of Pentecost, celebrates a new covenant: "I will make a new covenant with [you]..." (Jer. 31:31). The new covenant is God's holy law written on our hearts by the presence and power of His Holy Spirit!

The details of the Feast of Pentecost are as riveting as the details of the Passover celebration. The Hebrew name for this festival is *Shavuot* ("weeks")—a festival *seven weeks* after Firstfruits. "Firstfruits," according to Leviticus 23:9-11, is the waving of "a sheaf of the first grain you harvest...before the Lord." This was done on "the day after the Sabbath," the Sunday following Passover—Resurrection Sunday. Pentecost itself prefigures the new covenant coming of the *Ruach Ha-Kodesh,* the Holy Spirit, leading to the birth of the new covenant Church. Similarly, Israel, "the church in the wilderness" (Acts 7:38 KJV), was birthed on that first Pentecost at Mount Sinai 50 days after the exodus from Egypt. Exodus 19:1 places Israel at Mount Sinai in the month Sivan (our mid-June), 50 days after the exodus.

Stephen brought these thoughts together in his statement about Moses:

> *This is he, that was* **in the church in the wilderness** *with the angel which spake to him* **in the mount Sina** [Sinai], *and with our fathers: who received the lively oracles* [the Ten Commandments] *to give unto us* (Acts 7:38 KJV).

Actually, some of the very phenomena that accompanied the giving of the Law at Sinai in Exodus 19:18 reappeared in the outpourings of the Holy Spirit in Acts 2:2-3 and 4:31 in the fire and the wind and the earthquake!

Traditionally, Psalm 67 was recited on each of the 49 days of the seven weeks between Firstfruits [Resurrection Sunday] and Shavuot [Pentecost]. In the Hebrew text this Psalm has seven words (one for each of the seven weeks) and 49 verses (one for each of the 49 days leading up to Shavuot). David, tradition tells us, was born and died on Shavuot, and Psalm 67 printed below is a Pentecostal Davidic psalm celebrating the triumph of the outpouring of God's grace upon Jews and Gentiles together.

> *May God be gracious to us* [Israel] *and bless us*
> *And make His face shine upon us, Selah*
> *That Your ways may be known on earth,*
> *Your salvation among all nations* [the Gentiles].
> *May the peoples* [Israel] *praise You, O God;*

May all the peoples praise You.
May the nations [the Gentiles] *be glad and sing for joy,*
For You rule the peoples [Israel] *justly and guide*
The nations of the earth [the Gentiles]. *Selah*
May the peoples [Israel] *praise You, O God;*
May all the peoples praise You.
Then the land will yield its harvest,
And God, our God, will bless us [Israel].
God will bless us,
And all the ends of the earth [the Gentile nations]
Will fear Him.

What a wonderful psalm written in the apostolic missionary spirit of the Book of Acts, with the blessings of salvation showered upon the Jews first and then also upon the Gentiles (see Rom. 1:16).

Traditionally, the people of Israel believed that when God spoke from Mount Sinai in Exodus 20, people from 70 different nations of the earth heard Him speak the words of that marvelous law in their own language. That tradition sheds understanding on Luke's words in Acts chapter 2:

> *Now there were staying in Jerusalem God-fearing Jews* **from every nation under heaven…each one heard them speaking in his own language.…** *Parthians, Medes and Elamites; residents of Mesopotamia, Judea and Cappadocia, Pontus and Asia, Phrygia and Pamphylia, Egypt and the parts of Libya near Cyrene; visitors from Rome (both Jews and converts to Judaism); Cretans and Arabs* [heard] *them* **declaring the wonders of God in** [their] **own tongues!** (Acts 2:5-6;9-11)

A very sobering fact, however, about the aftermath of that first Pentecost is revealed in Exodus 32. The tables of the law had just been given by God to Israel, but because the people almost immediately violated that law by their idolatry, Moses, in anger, "threw the tablets out of his hands, breaking them to pieces at the foot of the mountain" (Exod. 32:19). The result would be that on "that day about three thousand of the people died" (Exod. 32:28) as judgment fell on them for their sin. How different would be the aftermath of the new covenant Day of Pentecost when "about three thousand" (Acts 2:41) were *forgiven* of their most grievous sins (particularly in their delivering the Holy One over to death, see Acts 2:23). These were then raised to new *life* as they came up out of the waters of baptism, cleansed by the redeeming power in the Name of our Lord Jesus Christ!

Pentecost is a *"first day of the week"* celebration (Lev. 23:15). As such, it is like Firstfruits, which celebrated the resurrection of our Lord Jesus "on the first day of the week" (Lev. 23:11; John 20:1). Israel was commanded to *rest* on the seventh day, the Sabbath (see Lev. 23:3), but they were then commanded to *celebrate* on the first day of the week! For that reason, Sunday really should be spelled *Sonday,* for it is a day celebrating the Son whom "God has raised...to life," the Son who, "exalted to the right hand of God...has received from the Father the promised Holy Spirit and has poured out what you now see and hear" (Acts 2:32-33)! The emerging tradition of the early Church makes sense in this light—"On *the first day of the week* we came together to break bread" (Acts 20:7; see also 1 Cor. 16:2). The first day of the week holds great significance in the messianic plan of God. It is the day of the "triple light:" Jesus, the firstborn Light of all creation; Jesus, the Firstborn from the dead; and Jesus, the firstborn Son who baptizes the family of God in the Holy Spirit and fire (see Gen. 1:3-5; John 1:4,9; Luke 24:1; Col. 1:18; Matt. 3:11). Each of these events are "first day of the week" events.

THE TWO WAVE LOAVES

The centerpiece of the Festival of Weeks is the waving of the two leavened wheat loaves. "From wherever you live, bring two loaves made of two-tenths of an ephah [about 4 quarts] of fine flour, baked with yeast, as a wave offering of firstfruits to the Lord" (Lev. 23:17). This celebration would take place at God's place, the Tabernacle of His Glory. These two hefty wheat loaves were a symbol of the two tables of

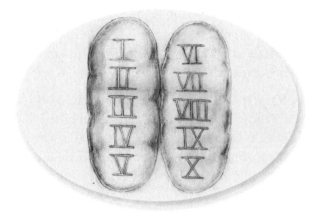

the Law. They were made from fine flour, *baked with leaven* (a picture of sin *arrested in its activity by the fire).*

Because Passover focused solely on Jesus, the *sinless* Lamb of God, the bread of that festival *had to be unleavened.* But because Pentecost involves *us* as the Spirit-baptized people of God, *there must be leaven* because that is exactly who we are—sinners in whom the fire of God is doing its work of arresting the leaven, the activity of sin!

The two loaves were a *wave offering.* The Hebrew word translated "wave" means "to rock to and fro, as a drunken man," giving deeper understanding to Peter's needed explanation: "These men are not *drunk, as you suppose...*" (Acts 2:15). The first Pentecostals were a living example of these original wheat loaves, waved (rocked to and fro like a drunken man) before the Lord as they were offered to Him as a consecrated offering!

Finally, Pentecost was called the "Feast of Harvest" (Exod. 23:16). Pentecost celebrated the spring grain harvest that was made possible by "the spring rains that water the earth" (Hos. 6:3; Joel 2:23; James 5:7). The outpouring of the Holy Spirit on the Day of Pentecost was the falling of the spring rain from Heaven and great was the harvest that was reaped as a result (see Acts 2:41,47; 4:4; 5:14; 6:1,7)!

The final significant words of Scripture detailing the Feast of Pentecost are these:

*When you reap the harvest of your land, do not reap to the very edges of your field or gather the gleanings of your harvest. **Leave them for the poor and the alien.** I am the Lord your God* (Leviticus 23:22).

True Pentecost will always create true community—community where there is an acute awareness of the needs of others and an impassioned commitment to see those needs met. That is why following the Pentecostal outpouring of Acts 2:44-45, we read these words: "All the believers were together and had everything in common. Selling their possessions and goods, *they gave to anyone as he had need*." And again in Acts 4:32: "All the believers were one in heart and mind. No one claimed that any of his possessions was his own, but *they shared everything they had*."

The festivals of Passover and Pentecost, the spring festivals, speak to us of the work of our Lord Jesus in His first coming. They were followed in turn by the long dry season of summer when often only the falling dew sustained life. This becomes such a clear picture of the history of the Church. Between the first and second comings of our Lord Jesus there has been a long, hot, dry season, but the true Church has been sustained by the falling dew—those ongoing seasons of refreshing from the Presence of the Lord (see Acts 3:19) that clearly mark the 2,000 year revival history of the Church.

This being gloriously true, we now turn our eyes toward the fall of the year and the times of the autumn rains and the time of the grand harvest of the oil and the wine called "the Feast of Ingathering at the end of the year" (Exod. 23:16). This will be our next consideration as we focus on the times and events leading up to the *Second* Coming of our Lord Jesus Christ.

PRAYER OF CONSECRATION

Spirit of the Living God, fall afresh on me! Write on my heart the holy law of my God. Exalt Jesus in my life and through my witness, I pray. Empower me, Lord of the

Harvest, to reap a precious harvest of souls for the glory of the Father. I yield myself to You! I lay my life before You in Jesus' wonderful Name. Amen.

Chapter 14

The Fall Festivals

THESE final festivals, the fall festivals of the Lord, are called by several names. In Exodus 23:16 the whole celebration is called *"The Feast of Ingathering* at the end of the year, when you gather in your crops from the field." This final celebration was held "in the seventh month," seven being the number of completion, for in this month our God will complete all things for His people!

There is but one fall celebration, "the Ingathering," but like its spring counterpart, Passover, it is made up of three festivals. The three component parts of the Ingathering are described for us in Leviticus 23:23-43.

First, there was the Festival of Trumpets—the Day of Trumpet Blasts (see Lev. 23:24). We will shortly consider this day of God's awakening call in more detail.

Second, there was the Day of Atonement. "The tenth day of this seventh month is *the Day of Atonement*…when atonement is made for you before the Lord your God" (Lev. 23: 27-28). We will also study this awesome day of cleansing and redemption in more detail.

The third celebration of this final feast is called "the Lord's Feast of Tabernacles." In the days of the olive and grape harvest, "on the fifteenth day of the seventh month the *Lord's Feast of Tabernacles* begins, and it lasts for seven days" (Lev. 23:34). For seven days the people of

God were to "live in booths," or tabernacles made from tree branches. The final day of this celebration called "the last and greatest day of the Feast" featured a special event thanking Jehovah for the fall rains—a celebration marked by the pouring out of water in the House of God, prefiguring the outpouring of God's Holy Spirit upon the Church of our Lord Jesus Christ. This celebration was followed by yet another special "add-on" celebration called *Simchat Torah*, "rejoicing in the Torah," actually a wedding celebration, declaring the joy of God's people in their union with the Torah, the holy law of God.

Harvest rains! A great ingathering! A wedding celebration! These are all dynamic end-time truths surrounding the Second Coming of our Lord Jesus Christ. And these are the themes of this third celebration of Ingathering with its multiple festivals.

First, the Festival of Trumpets

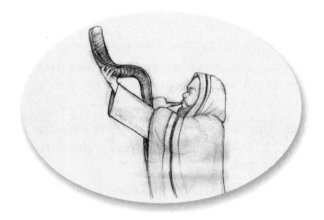

"On the first day of the seventh month you are to have a day of rest, a sacred assembly ['a rehearsal,' lit.] commemorated with *trumpet blasts*" (Lev. 23:24). The Hebrew for the expression "day of trumpet blasts" is *Yom Teruah*; literally, "the day of *awakening* trumpet blasts." Yom Teruah was celebrated on the first day of the seventh month, preceded by 30 days of repentance. Yom Teruah was then to be followed by "10 days of awe" in soul-searching preparation for Yom Kippur, the Day of Atonement. In Israel's calendar it became another, a second new year—the civil new year—and was called *Rosh Ha Shana* which literally means "Head of the Year." Jewish tradition claims this day to be the day on which Adam was created.

Some Bible interpreters, eager to get the predominantly Gentile Church off the scene so that God can bring natural Israel to the forefront, interpret Yom Teruah as the "trumpet call of God" of First Thessalonians 4:16, heralding the rapture of the Church. Paul's understanding, however, of the relationship between Israel and the Church as together being God's "one new man," Christ's "one body" (Eph. 2:15-16), does not allow for us to so divide Israel from the Church. Paul sees the Gentiles as *"heirs together* with Israel, *members together* of one body, and *sharers together* in the promise in Christ Jesus" (Eph. 3:6). Consequently, Paul's revelation of Israel's end-time restoration in Romans chapter 11 is not a restoration to be a *Kingdom separate* from the Church, but rather a restoration back into Israel's original olive tree into which the Gentiles have, by God's mercy, already been grafted—both together to partake of the rich root of Abraham, Isaac, and Jacob! Paul writes to the Gentile Romans:

> *After all, if you were cut out of an olive tree that is wild by nature, and contrary to nature were grafted into a cultivated olive tree, how much more readily will these, the natural branches, be grafted into their own olive tree!* (Romans 11:24).

The destinies of the Church and Israel are thus intertwined in the last days!

We must, therefore, see something other than First Thessalonians 4:16 in the "awakening trumpet blasts" of Yom Teruah. First of all, we notice it is *a series of "trumpet blasts,"* not just one "trumpet call" as in First Thessalonians 4:16. The purpose of these repeated trumpet blasts lies in that they are *"awakening* trumpet blasts"—trumpet blasts for the purpose of *waking up* a slumbering people and preparing them for the important end-time events that will soon follow. Paul probably had Yom Teruah in mind when he wrote to the Romans:

*And do this, understanding the present [kairos, lit.] time. The hour has come for you to **wake up from your slumber**, because our salvation is nearer now than when we first believed. The night is nearly over; the day is almost here. So let us put aside the deeds of darkness and put on the armor of light* (Romans 13:11-12).

To those who have an ear to hear what the Spirit is saying, these days *today* are clearly prophetic days of an awakening call—days of great awakening, preparing the people of God for the final chapters of human history!

Second, The Day of Atonement

The tenth day of this seventh month is the Day of Atonement. Hold a sacred assembly and deny [humble or "afflict," KJV] yourselves, and present an offering made to the Lord by fire (Leviticus 23:27).

The Hebrew expression for "Day of Atonement" is *Yom Kippur* or *Yom Ha Kippurim,* "Day of Atonement" or "Day of the Covering." The centerpiece of the entire month-long fall celebration of Ingathering is *this one day*—the Day of Atonement. This is evidenced by the fact that the entire chapter of Leviticus 16 is devoted to *this one day* in the seventh month on the tenth day of the month!

Amidst the various sacrifices offered on that day, the centerpiece of the Day of Atonement itself was when Aaron, washed with pure water and clothed in holy linen garments, took two male goats for a sin offering and presented them before the Lord at the entrance to the Tent of Meeting. He then cast lots for the two goats: one lot for the Lord and the other for the scapegoat, "the goat of removal," "the goat for sending away" (lit.).

*Aaron shall bring the goat whose lot falls to the Lord and sacrifice it for a sin offering. But the goat chosen by lot as the scapegoat shall be presented alive before the Lord **to be used for making atonement** by sending it into the desert as a scapegoat* (Leviticus 16:9-10).

Some have interpreted the scapegoat, the goat of removal, as satan. But this is not supported by the biblical statement, *"the scapegoat shall be...used for making atonement...."* No serious student of Scripture would ever include satan in the atonement! The atonement comes *only* through our Lord Jesus Christ and Him *alone*. How then can we understand the two goats?

In Leviticus 14:1-7 we have a parallel type, but instead of two goats we have two birds.

*The priest shall order that **one of the birds be killed** over fresh water in a clay pot. He is then to take the live bird and dip it...into the blood of the bird that was killed over the fresh water....Then he is to **release the live bird in the open fields*** (Leviticus 14:5-7).

Two goats—one sacrificed and the other released in the desert; two birds—one killed and the other released in the open fields. In both of these types we see Jesus in the two aspects of His redeeming work—in His death and in His resurrection. In His death He is the atoning sacrifice whose blood cleanses away our transgressions; in His resurrection He is the living Lord, raised for our justification. In Romans 4:25 Paul presents these two aspects of our Lord's saving work:

He was delivered over to death for our sins [like the slain bird and like the sacrificed goat] *and was raised to life for our* justification [like the live bird released in the open fields, and the live goat released in the desert].

Well may we wonder if Paul did not have Leviticus chapter 16 in mind when he wrote those words to the Romans!

Aaron was to:

...slaughter the goat for the sin offering for the people and take its blood behind the curtain and...sprinkle it on the atonement cover ["the mercy seat," KJV] and in front of it. In this way he will make atonement for the Most Holy Place because of the uncleanness and rebellion of the Israelites, whatever their sins have been.... No one is to be in the Tent of Meeting from the time Aaron goes in to make atonement in the Most Holy Place until he comes out, having made atonement for himself, his household and the whole community of Israel (Leviticus 16:15-17).

What a breathtaking event!

Then began the elaborate ceremony regarding the live goat, the goat of removal.

*When Aaron has finished making atonement for the Most Holy Place, the Tent of Meeting and the altar, he shall bring forward the live goat. He is to lay both hands on the head of the live goat **and confess over it all the wickedness and rebellion of the Israelites—all their sins—and put them on the goat's head.** He shall send the goat away into the desert in the care of a man appointed for the task. **The goat will carry on itself all their sins** to a solitary place; and the man shall release it in the desert (Leviticus 16:20-22).*

This great substitution can *only* be a picture of our Lord Jesus Christ who "takes away the sins of the world" (John 1:29). Yes, Christ "has appeared once for all at the end of the ages *to do away with sin by the sacrifice of Himself*" (Heb. 9:26). Praise God!

There is a Jewish tradition that tells how a crimson sash was attached to the door of the Temple at Jerusalem on Yom Kippur at the same time that the scapegoat with a similar crimson cord attached to one of its horns was sent into the wilderness. The temple sash would consistently turn from red to white indicating the atonement sacrifice had been accepted and sins were forgiven—for "though your sins are like scarlet, they shall be white as snow" (Isa. 1:18). Forty years before the A.D. 70 destruction of the Temple by Titus (around A.D. 30) the red temple sash *stopped turning white.*[1] The goat was *no longer accepted by God* as an atonement for sins because the Messiah was now coming to make the final atonement for sin by His death on the cross!

Every 50 years in the history of God's people, the year of Jubilee *began on the Day of Atonement;* Jubilee was a year in which the captives were set free!

> *Have the trumpet sounded everywhere on the tenth day of the seventh month;* **on the Day of Atonement** *sound the trumpet throughout your land. Consecrate the fiftieth year and* **proclaim liberty throughout the land to all its inhabitants.** *It shall be a jubilee for you.... In this year of Jubilee everyone is to return to his own property* (Leviticus 25:9-10;13).

Since Adam, around 4000 B.C., until now, approximately A.D. 2000, 6,000 years have gone by, or *120* years of Jubilee (120 × 50 = 6,000)! And *120* is a very significant number in the visitation of the Holy Spirit upon the people of God (see 2 Chron. 5:12-14 and Acts 1:15; 2:1-2).

We need also to note here that inscribed on the Liberty Bell in Philadelphia are these words of Jubilee: "Proclaim liberty throughout the land...." That inscription, celebrating Jubilee, would be a prophetic statement for the United States of America. For every 50 years, starting with the Great Awakening in the mid-1700s, the United States would experience an unusual outpouring of the Holy Spirit, resulting in setting captives free!

The Great Awakening of the 1750s was followed by the Second Great Awakening of the late 1700s and early 1800s...which was followed by the Great Outpourings under Charles G. Finney and others in the mid-1800s...which was followed by the Welsh Revival of 1904 and Azusa Street in 1906...which was followed by the Latter Rain and the Healing Revivals in the mid-1900s...which birthed the Charismatic Move of the 1960s, 1970s, and 1980s, and in turn the Toronto Blessing and Pensacola Revival in the 1990s. And now we await yet another outpouring in these early years of 2000!

One final and important thought concerning the Day of Atonement: "On the tenth day of the seventh month you must...*not do any work....* It is *a sabbath of rest*" (Lev. 16:29,31). The command in Leviticus chapter 23 is even more emphatic:

> **Do no work** on that day, because it is the Day of Atonement....
> **I will destroy from among his people anyone who does
> any work on that day.** You shall **do no work at all....** It is **a
> sabbath of rest** for you... (Leviticus 23:28;30-32).

Hebrews 4:10-11 helps us to understand why this issue of rest is of such deep importance: "Anyone who enters God's rest also *rests from his own work....* Let us, therefore, make every effort *to enter that rest...*" The work of Jesus on the cross and the atonement that He thereby procured for us *precludes any work on our part.* His work is *a finished work!* From the cross He shouted with a loud voice: "It is finished!" (John 19:30) The phrase "it is finished" is actually one word in the Greek New Testament—*tetelestai,* a verb in the perfect tense, meaning "it is finished and *remains* finished—completed, consummated, and perfected forever, and its infinite results continue through all time and eternity, effectual for all..." (from Boyce Blackwelder, Greek scholar and author).[2] Hallelujah! We can bring *nothing* into the salvation equation. It is *all* His work, and ours is to *rest* in the awesome finished work of our Lord Jesus Christ! This is the message of the Day of Atonement.

And at the end of the age in the last days God will bring His people into a new and dynamic experience of the atonement of Jesus. The ground on which we will be able to stand in the last days in the face of all the accusations of the devil—that ground will only be *the blood of the Lamb!* "They overcame him [satan] *by the blood of the Lamb...*" (Rev. 12:11). Amen! That is why the Day of Atonement is the centerpiece of this whole Fall Celebration, because the atonement of Jesus is the sole, solid ground on which both Israel and the Gentiles will be able to stand in the last days.

PRAYER OF CONSECRATION

Father, I hear the prophetic, awakening trumpet blasts! I do rise up from my slumber to put on the whole armor of God. Prepare my heart for these last days, O God.

Lord Jesus Christ, I thank You for Your blood which will never lose its power. Thank You for Your finished work! You have died for my sins, and You have carried them far, far away. I stand in these last days under the shelter of Your blood, to see the enemy overcome by its might and its power.

Spirit of the Lord, energize my life that the word of my testimony will be bright and clear as I love not my life, even to death! In Jesus' Name. Amen.

ENDNOTES

1. Eddie Chumney, *The Seven Festivals of the Messiah* (Shippensburg, PA: Destiny Image Publishers, 1994), p. 66. Chumney refers to this tradition being in the Mishna. The same observation is made in the magazine *Israel My Glory* (August/September 1991), p. 8.

2. Boyce W. Blackwelder, *Light From the Greek New Testament* (Grand Rapids, MI: Baker Book House, 1958), p. 69.

Chapter 15

THE FESTIVAL
OF TABERNACLES

THE Festival of Tabernacles is called *Succoth* in the Hebrew language, meaning booths or tabernacles—temporary dwelling places for pilgrims to live in. The Festival of Tabernacles, Succoth, was the third of the three Fall Festivals—first *Yom Teruah*, then *Yom Kippur*, and now *Succoth*. Interestingly, within this third and final Festival of Succoth itself are found *three mini-celebrations*—the seven days of *dwelling in booths* followed by *Simchat Beit Ha Shoevah* ("rejoicing in the house of the water pouring"), followed by *Simchat Torah*, a glorious wedding celebration.

All of these fall happenings so clearly speak to us of the events surrounding the Second Coming of our Lord Jesus Christ even as the happenings of the two spring celebrations—Passover and Pentecost—speak to us of the events surrounding His first coming. These three annual celebrations in all their component parts are *all about Jesus* and the work He accomplishes in His first and second comings. Such an awesome prophetic panorama is found in these amazing festivals! And to think that all these "parties" took place at God's house, at His place: His people celebrating before Him in the Tabernacle of His Glory!

THE FOUR SPECIES

On the fifteenth day of the seventh month the Lord's Feast of Tabernacles begins, and it lasts for seven days...beginning with the fifteenth day of the seventh month, after you have gathered the crops of the land, celebrate the festival to the Lord for seven days....On the first day you are to take choice fruit [the citron] *from the trees, and palm fronds, leafy branches* [from the myrtle] *and poplars, and **rejoice before the Lord your God for seven days.** Celebrate this as a festival to the Lord for seven days each year...* (Leviticus 23:34;39-41).

This celebration of rejoicing centered around the waving before the Lord of "the Four Species" (as they came to be known). The "choice fruit," the citron, which had both fragrance and taste, was held in the left hand of the pilgrim, representing *the Gentiles.* The "palm fronds" held in the right hand represented *the Jews.* This species had just taste, but no fragrance. The "leafy branches," the myrtle, had fragrance but no taste and was also held in the right hand *representing the Jews.* The "poplars," having neither fragrance nor taste, were held in the right hand, also *representing the Jews.*[1] These four species were waved in celebration for seven days before the Lord, representing the offering up of both Jews and Gentiles to Him.

THE BOOTHS

The Lord then commanded:

Live in booths *for seven days: All native-born Israelites are to **live in booths** so your descendants will know that I had the Israelites **live in booths** when I brought them out of Egypt. I am the Lord your God* (Leviticus 23:42-43).

These pilgrim shelters were to be an ongoing reminder of the pilgrim status of God's people. Like the patriarchs, God's people were to be "aliens and strangers in [this] world," with no certain dwelling

place, "looking forward to the city with foundations, whose architect and builder is God" (1 Pet. 2:11; Heb. 11:10).

Deuteronomy 16:14-15 contains a most wonderful further ingredient of this festival—joy! This festival, Tabernacles, is the only festival that comes with *a command to be joyful!*

> ***Be joyful*** *at your Feast—you, your sons and daughters, your menservants and maidservants, and the Levites, the aliens, the fatherless and the widows who live in your towns....The Lord your God will bless you in all your harvest and in all the work of your hands, and **your joy will be complete.***

A similar statement in Nehemiah 8:10, "the joy of the Lord is your strength," was actually given in the context of the then newly rediscovered Festival of Tabernacles! The returned exiles began to "celebrate with great joy"—for "they found written in the Law, which the Lord commanded through Moses, that the Israelites were to live in booths during the feast of the seventh month" (Neh. 8:12,14). And so "the whole company that had returned from exile built booths ['on their own roofs, in their courtyards, in the courts of the house of God']. From the days of Joshua son of Nun until that day [about 1,000 years], the Israelites had not celebrated it like this. And *their joy was very great*" (Neh. 8:16-17). Succoth is the celebration of a blessed pilgrim people, *"filled with an inexpressible glorious joy"* (1 Pet. 1:8)!

THE FESTIVAL OF THE NATIONS

The Feast of Tabernacles has been called *the Festival of the Nations.* More than any other of the festivals, Succoth included in its pageantry the nations of the earth. We have already seen that in Israel's celebration of joy in using the four species, the choice fruit (the citron), which had both "fragrance and taste," traditionally spoke of *the Gentiles.* The three other species, each incomplete in themselves, spoke of Israel. In this ritual we have a subtle hint of the plan of God for Israel—"God had planned…that only *together with us* would *they* be made perfect" (a thought borrowed from Hebrews 11:40).

The most pronounced emphasis on the nations, however, is found in the ritual recorded in Numbers 29:12-38. Over eight days of celebration, 71 bulls, representing Israel and the Gentiles, were offered as burnt offerings before the Lord, along with "…two rams and fourteen male lambs a year old, all without defect" (Num. 29:13). On the first of the eight days *"thirteen* young bulls" were offered (29:13); on the second day, *"twelve* young bulls (29:17); on the third day, *"eleven* bulls" (24:20); on the fourth day *"ten* bulls" (29:23); on the fifth day, *"nine* bulls" (29:26); on the sixth day, *"eight* bulls" (29:29); on the seventh day *"seven* bulls" (29:32)—a grand total of 70 bulls. These bulls represent the Gentiles and are listed in a diminishing order, for Messiah "must become greater," and the world "must become less" (John 3:30). Then on the eighth day, "a burnt offering of *one* bull" was offered to the Lord (Num. 29:36).

Our inquiry into the 70 bulls plus the one additional bull is revealing. Deuteronomy 32:8, speaking of the known world that surrounded Israel, states that "when the Most High gave the nations their inheritance, when He divided all mankind, He set up boundaries for the peoples *according to the number of the sons of Israel.*" Exodus 1:5 states that the number of the sons of Israel who went down into Egypt was *"seventy in all,"* inclusive of Joseph and his family. From these Scriptures the deduction was made from Deuteronomy 32:8 that there were *70 Gentile nations* (the same number as the sons of Israel) surrounding Israel in the then known world. All of these 70 nations, it was believed, heard the Law of God in their own language when God thundered from Mt. Sinai on that original Day of Pentecost! And now all 70 of them would be represented by the 70 bulls offered up before the Lord as burnt offerings over these seven days of Succoth!

This may be what Paul had in mind when he wrote to the Romans about his calling:

> ...*to be a minister of Christ Jesus to the Gentiles with the priestly duty of proclaiming the gospel of God, so that* **the Gentiles might become an offering acceptable to God,** *sanctified by the Holy Spirit* (Romans 15:16).

On the eighth day one solitary bull was offered as a burnt offering to the Lord, representing *the singular nation of Israel,* so the whole world was accounted for in these sacrifices of consecration—Israel and the Gentiles together!

Tabernacles is mentioned more by the prophets than all the other feasts combined, pointing to its end-time significance, as "the survivors from all the nations that have attacked Jerusalem will go up year after year to worship the King, the Lord Almighty, and *to celebrate the Feast of Tabernacles*" (Zech. 14:16). Syria and the Saudis will be there, and Iraq and Iran will be there, and all who have hated Israel will come. O, glorious Kingdom day when "the Lord will be *King over the whole earth.* On that day there will be one Lord, and His name the only name" (Zech. 14:9)!

The New Testament celebrates the fullness of this revelation in these words written by John:

> *I looked and there before me was* **a great multitude that no one could count,** *from* **every** *nation, tribe, people and language, standing before the throne and in front of the Lamb. They were wearing white robes and were holding palm branches in their hands. And they cried out in a loud voice: "Salvation belongs to our God, who sits on the throne, and to the Lamb"* (Revelation 7:9-10).

Along with the redeemed from Israel (see Rev. 7:4-8) will be these multitudes from among the Gentiles all celebrating Succoth together, "holding palm branches in their hands," and glorifying the Lamb who was slain for their salvation! This is the true fulfillment of the Feast of Tabernacles!

A Glorious End-time Harvest

The predominant note in the Feast of Tabernacles was *harvest*— a celebration of *the final harvest* at the end of the year—speaking so clearly of the final glorious end-time harvest from among Jews and Gentiles that precedes the Second Coming of our Lord Jesus Christ. "…Celebrate the Feast of Ingathering *at the end of the year, when you gather in your crops* from the field" (Exod. 23:16). "Beginning with the fifteenth day of the seventh month, *after you have gathered the crops of the land,* celebrate the festival to the Lord…" (Lev. 23:39). "Celebrate the Feast of Tabernacles for seven days *after you have gathered the produce of your threshing floor and your wine press*" (Deut. 16:13).

This festival itself is called "the Feast of *Ingathering*"—and what an ingathering it shall be!

> And they sang a new song: "You are worthy…because You were slain, and with Your blood You purchased men…**from every tribe and language and people and nation.** You have made them to be a kingdom and priests to serve our God, and they will reign on the earth" (Revelation 5:9-10).

Statisticians tell us that by the end of the first century one out of every 360 people on earth were confessing Christians. By 1950 (the year that I was born again as a teenager in Brooklyn, New York), *one out of every 20* people on earth were confessing Christians! But by the year 2000 with a world population of 6 billion people—twice that of 1950— *one out of every six people* on earth were confessing Christians![2]

A harvest is maturing in the fields before our very eyes, and that harvest is being gathered for the Lord in these final days! "Do you not say, 'Four months more and then the harvest'? I tell you, *open your eyes and look at the fields! They are ripe for harvest*" (John 4:35). We have a mandate from God to "speed [the] coming" of the day of God (2 Pet. 3:12)! And Jesus told us exactly *how* we can do that—"And this gospel of the kingdom will be preached in the whole world as a testimony to all nations [to all ethnic groups, literally], and *then* the end will come" (Matt. 24:14)!

"Do No Regular Work"

A most unusual phrase appears and reappears in the mandates that surround Succoth, the Feast of Ingathering, the celebration of the harvest: "Do *no regular work*" (Lev. 23:35-36; Num. 29:12). "Do *no regular work*"! "Do *no regular work*"! "Business as usual" has no part in this great harvest. Conventional ways and normal means will not work. These are days of *supernatural* happenings! "Wonders in the heaven above and signs on the earth below..." (Acts 2:19). These are days when God takes over the work as never before. That is the only way to account for the abundance of harvest that we are seeing in all the earth in these days. This is fast becoming the grandest harvest this world has ever seen—"*a great multitude that no one could count* from every nation, tribe, people and language...." Praise God!

Two "Add-on" Festivals

The detailed instructions of Moses for the Festival of Ingathering *conclude* with Israel living for seven days in booths (see Lev. 23:42). Passing mention is made to an "eighth day" (*Shemini Atzeret*, meaning the eighth festive assembly) after the seven days of living in booths: "On *the eighth day* hold a sacred assembly and present an offering made to the Lord by fire. It is *the closing assembly; do no regular work*" (Lev. 23:36). "Celebrate the festival to the Lord for seven days; the first day is a day of rest, and *the eighth day* also is a day of rest" (Lev. 23:39).

By the time of Jesus, the concluding day of Tabernacles had itself become a full-blown festival, an "add-on" festival that took place "on the last and greatest day of the Feast..." (John 7:37). This festival was called *Simchat Beit Ha Shoevah,* which means "rejoicing in the house of the water pouring." A golden pitcher of water was drawn from the Gihon Spring by the high priest and poured out in the Temple along with a libation of wine, all in celebration of the faithfulness of God in sending the abundant autumn rains that had brought the fruit harvest to perfection.

It was at that very moment of celebration:

> *On the last and greatest day of the Feast* [that] *Jesus stood and said in a loud voice* ["shouted," lit.]*, "If anyone is thirsty let him come to Me and drink. Whoever believes in Me, as the Scripture has said, streams of living water will flow* ['gush forth,' lit] *from within him." By this He meant the Spirit, whom those who believed in Him were later to receive...* (John 7:37-39).

The Scripture referred to by Jesus in His statement, "as the Scripture has said," may be Isaiah 12:3: "*With joy* you will draw water from the wells of salvation," for this was one of the most joyful times on Israel's calendar. The Talmud comments: "He who has not seen the rejoicing at the place of the water-drawing *has never seen rejoicing in his life.*" Another Scripture Jesus may have had in mind on that day is the beautiful description of the bride in Song of Songs 4:15: "You are a garden fountain, a well of flowing ['*living*,' KJV] *water* streaming down from Lebanon." This indeed was *Hoshana Rabbah* ("the great salvation")!

The utter ecstasy and joy of the Water Pouring Festival is described in the *Mishnah* as a colorful, joyful, and even riotous celebration! The *Talmud* (in *Sukkah* 5:1) describes people juggling lighted torches and performing somersaults, expressing their ecstatic joy!

Priests cut down long willow branches and walked row after row, swishing their willow branches back and forth, making a rushing sound as they approached the Temple, along with the high priest carrying the golden pitcher of water and another the silver pitcher of wine. The whole procession was led by a solitary flute player called "the pierced one"—a picture of the crucified Messiah who declared, "they have *pierced* My hands and My feet" (Ps. 22:16), the One who "was *pierced* for our transgressions" (Isa. 53:5), the One of whom Zechariah speaks: "They will look on Me, the One they have *pierced,* and they will mourn for Him..." (Zech. 12:10). The pierced one, the swishing willows, and the pitchers of water and wine to be poured out on the altar are all symbols of the pierced Messiah bringing the rushing wind of the Spirit, the outpouring of the Living Water, into the House of God in the last days.

Another amazing part of this celebration was the illumination of the Temple. Four enormous golden candlesticks were lit in the Court of the Women. The light emanating from the candlesticks was so bright, according to the *Mishnah,* that there was no courtyard in Jerusalem that was not lit with light on that day![3] According to Jewish tradition, the cloudy pillar of fire, the Shekinah Glory, first appeared to Israel on this very day in the Feast of Tabernacles, and the Shekinah Glory also came to Solomon's Temple on this very day during this Feast. This extraordinary illumination celebrated that Shekinah Glory! And on that very day Jesus declared of Himself, *"I am the light of the world. Whoever follows Me will never walk in darkness, but will have the light of life"* (John 8:12).

THE FINAL, FINAL FESTIVAL

The eighth day, "the last and greatest day of the Feast...," over time gave birth to yet another festivity, which we can call the *final, final* celebration of the Feast: *Simchat Torah,* the "Rejoicing in the Torah."

Because of my own personal experience of Simchat Torah many years ago in Tiberias, Israel, the festivals of the Lord began to open up to me, and I began the pursuit to understand them more clearly—a pursuit that has brought me to this writing at this time.

I was sitting on the balcony of our hotel room in Tiberias, over-looking the beautiful Sea of Galilee. To my left, at street level, I could actually see into the window of what I later discovered was a small synagogue, and what I saw amazed me! I saw people rejoicing, dancing in a circle, shouting with glee! I put on my yarmulke, went down to the street, found the entrance to the little synagogue, and presented myself at the door. I was quickly ushered into the main meeting room and just as quickly found myself dancing with the others in a circle around a rabbi holding a Torah scroll!

I watched as different ones touched the scroll in awe. Some kissed the scroll with deep affection. I was amazed! Though I did not at the time know what I was witnessing, I could only think—this is how the Jewish people will respond when they see Jesus in His Second Coming—touching Him in awe, kissing Him in delight (see Ps. 2:12), dancing around Him in wonder! I later discovered that I was witness-ing the final, final festival of the Feast of Tabernacles—Simchat Torah, the "Rejoicing in the Torah."

Bruce Scott in his article "Simchat Torah" in *Israel My Glory*, September 1991, wrote:

> "One of the happiest of all Jewish holidays is Simchat Torah (Rejoicing over the Law)…this delightful holiday has but one word to describe it—joy. There is joy in the home.

There is joy in the synagogue. There is joy throughout the entire Jewish community."

Amazingly, Scott points out, one of the readers of the Torah scroll is called *"the Bridegroom."* Bruce Scott observes, "The day is drawn to a close with *the Bridegroom of the Torah* providing a sumptuous feast for the entire congregation."[4]

In his book *The Feasts of the Lord*, Ron Cantrell also describes Simchat Torah as having "a distinctive wedding flavor." He likewise observes:

> "The reception ceremony for a new Torah scroll…is called Hachatunat Sefer Torah [meaning 'the Wedding Book of the Torah']…[and that] the celebration is more like a wedding ceremony and reception [as] men and boys, some with large blazing torches, head up a long parade following a chuppa (a prayer shawl tacked to four tall poles to create a wedding canopy), with the new scroll under it. Just as in a wedding, the chuppa sheltered the new Torah scroll."[5]

Though Simchat Torah was not originally a part of the Feast of Tabernacles as given by God through Moses, it has become one of those blessed "add-on" festivals. And we can actually see a resemblance of Simchat Torah in what is described in Revelation chapter 19. Here the bride is the Jewish-Gentile Church and the Bridegroom is our Lord Jesus, who bears the name "the Word of God" (Rev. 19:13)—the new Torah. This is the blessed marriage of the Word of God to the people of God! And this is the way these wonderful celebrations at God's Place concluded:

> *"Let us rejoice and be glad and give* [God] *glory! For the wedding of the Lamb has come, and His bride has made herself ready. Fine linen, bright and clean, was given her to wear."* (Fine linen stands for the righteous acts ["the righteousness," KJV] of the saints)….*I saw heaven standing open and there before me was a white horse, whose rider is called Faithful and True. With justice He judges and makes*

*war. His eyes are like blazing fire, and on His head are many crowns. He has a name written on Him that no one knows but He Himself. He is dressed in a robe dipped in blood, and His name is **the Word of God**. The armies of heaven were following Him, riding on white horses and dressed in fine linen, white and clean....On His robe and on His thigh He has this name written: King of Kings and Lord of Lords* (Revelation 19:7-8;11-14;16)!

Hallelujah! This is where the redemption of Passover and the fullness of Pentecost have brought us! Now this is the climax of the multifaceted Feast of Ingathering. This is the end, the consummation, the finale of all things! Our Lord will reign as King of all kings and Lord of all lords! And we shall be with Him, as His bride, forever by His side.

The copious autumn rains have fallen. The grand harvest of the earth has been safely gathered in. The wedding of the people of God—Jew and Gentile—to the Living Word of God has taken place. And now eternity—in all of its awesome majesty—begins. Our Lord Jesus Christ shall reign forever and ever! Hallelujah and Amen!

PRAYER OF CONSECRATION

Holy God, Father, Son, and Holy Spirit, Your people are willing in the day of Your power, and by Your grace I offer myself to You as a living sacrifice in this hour! Take my life, in all that I am and in all that I ever hope to be, and use my life in these momentous days for Your glory. Use me in the harvest; use me in the ingathering; use me in the outpouring. Here am I, O Lord! Send me, I humbly pray in Jesus' Name. Amen.

ENDNOTE

1. Eddie Chumney, *The Seven Festivals of the Messiah* (Shippensburg, PA: Destiny Image Publishers, 1994), p. 81.

2. According to *Operation World* (2004), there are 2 billion Christians worldwide out of a total population of 6 billion. That means that 33% of the world, that's 2 out of every 6 people, are Christians. I went on the belief that half of these were confessing Christians, which is why I used the statistic of 1 in 6.

3. This is referred to in the *Israel My Glory* magazine (August/September 1991), p. 11. In *The Seven Festivals of the Messiah,* Eddie Chumney states the same, quoting the Mishha (Sukkah 5:3).

4. Bruce Scott, "Simchat Torah," *Israel My Glory* (August/September 1991), p. 13.

5. Ron Cantrell, *The Feast of the Lord* (Tulsa, OK: Bridges for Peace, 1999), p. 85-86.

For more information about
Charles P. Schmitt, visit:

www.immanuels.org